Writing the College

Essay

Niaz Khan

wp
Whittier Publications, Inc.

Published by Whittier Publications, Inc.
Island Park, NY 11558

ISBN 1-57604-277-4

Printed in the United States of America

10 9 8 7 6 5 4 3 2 1 0

Preface

Majority of the students entering college have little knowledge about writing a five-paragraph essay. One told me that she had no idea that an essay for a composition course should be in the five-paragraph format. I have been teaching writing for a number of years, and I am noticing that writing skills are on the decline. A large number of students care very little because they feel their majors or career choices will rarely need good writing skills. However, it is a fact that employers are seeking employees with excellent communication skills, both oral and written. Engineers need to learn to write well, so do nurses and people in almost every profession. It is disconcerting to note many who are entering the teaching profession also have serious shortcomings in composition skills. On many sleepless nights I have wondered why students are unable to write coherent, well organized, and grammatically correct essays. A number of my colleagues blame school teachers. Many blame the video game industry. Others blame the students for their lackadaisical attitude. Whoever or whatever is to blame does not matter. The task for English professors is to prepare their students to succeed in their educational, professional, and personal endeavors. As a result, composition needs to be taught as a process in easy steps.

Nearly all of the textbooks for the teaching and learning of writing skills are densely written, which make it uninteresting to the students. This book intends to make the process simpler and more appealing. I teach my students to follow the KISS (Keep It Simple Stupid) principle, which I have endeavored to follow in this work. Simplicity is the hallmark of good communication. The book leads the student in a chronological manner to the end product, a finely crafted essay. If students adhere to the steps I have set out on prewriting, writing, and rewriting, they would by the end of the semester become comfortable in creating the five-paragraph essay. I have emphasized that the delineated steps must be strictly followed. At the beginning, students will complain about the process because most of them are not used to meticulously following guidelines. The steps, however, become routine by the end of the semester. A composition course usually requires seven essays.

The book is divided into five sections: Prewriting, Writing, Rewriting, Plagiarism, and Problems Areas: Grammar, Punctuation, Mechanics, and Others. I felt the need to say a few words about plagiarism, so I put it separately in Section V of the book. Lately, plagiarism has been showing up consistently in student papers, especially with the advent of the Internet. In the last chapter I have provided a review of errors frequently found in the composition of new writers. Those problems are explained and supplemented with ways to correct them. Students are generally required to write seven essays in the first college composition course. Accordingly, I have enclosed a tracking chart (Errors Chart List) that would be useful to both the students and their professors. Students tear it and enclose it with every essay they turn in. In turn, the professors mark in each column of the seven essays the major errors and grade in that particular assignment. At a glance students and professors can see the progress, or lack thereof, of writing skills. By mastering the art of composing a five-paragraph essay, students can move onto other types of writing—research papers, critiques, abstracts, journals, and others. A sequel to this book is the *Writing the College Research Paper.*

Without the encouragement of people close to me the writing of this book would not have been possible. I will start by thanking my oldest sister Perveen Shahjahan of the University of Arkansas at Pine Bluff for looking at my manuscript and giving me valuable advice. Her husband Mirza Shahjahan always motivated me to excel every one of my endeavors. Carol Mitchell Leon, my chairperson at Clark Atlanta University, gave me words of encouragement while I have been working on this book. Thanks to Karen Schein, the publisher's representative, who believed in me and did everything possible in the completion of this book. My editor Jerry Etra gets a very special thanks for helping me bring out the final product. I would be remiss not to mention my students because I have tested the contents of this book on them over the years. Now they will have an easier time becoming proficient writers by following my lectures on the pages of *Writing the College Essay.* The last group of people without whose support this book would not have been possible. That group is my family and they deserve my gratefulness: my wife Humaira and sons Ridwan and Imran. In fact, I took over Imran's computer when the laptop I was using became unavailable to me.

Table of Contents

1

Prewriting

sound foundation is the basis for a strong building. Long jumpers and high jumpers run up several feet before they take their jumps. Similarly, prewriting, or as some call it planning, is the first step in becoming a successful writer. This is a crucial first stage.

Sometimes you will be assigned a topic. At other times, you will have to find your own. Whatever the situation, you will begin with careful consideration of your audience, the assignment, the length, and knowledge of the topic. These factors will require you to think about your paper by not just giving a cursory thought but earnestly engaging in the process. That is brainstorming. Brainstorming is difficult. Most people shy away from it, saying, "I don't want to think about it now;" or "I'll think about it tomorrow." What happens is the onset of procrastination—the bane of human beings.

Brainstorming

Brainstorming is a must. Without participating in it, you will have a hard time coming up with the ingredients of the composition. In essence, brainstorming is the generating of ideas about the subject matter. Start brainstorming as soon as you settle on your topic. The trick is to write down all the ideas. A large number of successful writers keep a small notebook, something like a reporter's notebook, with them all the time—jotting down all of their inspirations. Do not count on your memory to retain whatever you have come up with. Another thing you ought to do is come up as many ideas as possible. The more you have, the better it is. Quantity is more important in this stage than quality. There are many ways of brainstorming: 1) listing, 2) clustering, mapping, or webbing, 3) freewriting, and 4) asking questions. Whichever method you prefer, use it.

Become proficient in it. Besides, turn in your brainstorming with your composition if your instructor asks you to do so. If not, keep your brainstorming in a three-ring binder or inside a manila envelope with all the material of that particular essay.

Listing

Many of us make "things to do lists," so we do not forget the tasks we have to accomplish. Going to the grocery store without a list is unthinkable for a number of us. (Of course, there are some who are impulsive shoppers.) Listing is simply writing down all that comes into the mind about the topic. Let us take topic the causes of divorce, which can generate a large number of ideas . Since almost 60 percent of American couples will get a divorce, this topic can produce a lot of ideas—some thirty or more. On a piece of paper, write down the title of your essay, if not the title, at least the subject matter and follow it with the ideas you have engendered in the following manner.

Causes of Divorce

Financial issues

Lack of communication

Lack of trust

Infidelity

...and other ideas

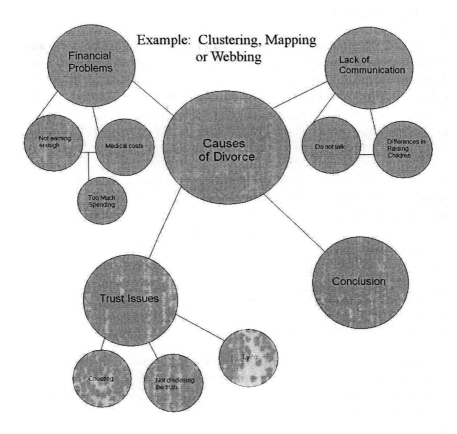

Clustering, Mapping, or Webbing

   Generally, those who are visual like to cluster, map, or web their ideas on a piece of paper—making it easier for them see the relationship or connectedness of ideas. You can put in practice this form of brainstorming by taking a clean sheet of paper and writing on the center the title or topic. Follow it up by drawing large ovals for the main ideas, connecting them and interconnecting with smaller ovals which contain sub-ideas. Words of caution, a topic like causes of divorce can become unwieldy because of its ability to generate a very large number of ideas. Therefore, do your clustering, mapping, or webbing carefully in such a situation. You can use the following as a model for this type of brainstorming.

Freewriting

Freewriting is a favorite means of brainstorming for countless students because they feel they can skip several steps in the writing process. According to them, freewriting is the prototype of the composition they will turn in. In other words, they fail to realize that this type of brainstorming also is responsible in churning out ideas. In freewriting, you set yourself a time limit, between 10 and 30 minutes, in which you write nonstop on the topic. If your mind stops working, do not stop writing. While freewriting on the causes of divorce, if your thoughts turn to Mickey Mouse as having been born in 1928, write down "Mickey Mouse was born in 1928." After you have exhausted your time limit, weed through what you have put down on paper. Pick those items that are only relevant to divorce, and discard the rest. This kind of brainstorming is by no means the easiest one.

Asking Questions

Another method of brainstorming is asking questions and answering them. This is the favorite method of reporters. Journalism schools teach their students to brainstorm by asking "WH" questions. "WH" questions can be another way you can come up with ideas for your composition. Answer these questions while being focused on the topic, and you will produce enough ideas to write your paper:

Who?

What?

When?

Where?

Why?

How?

Thesis Statement

After mulling through all the ideas you have spawned on the topic of the causes of divorce, choose three of the top reasons. In my view, they are financial problems, lack of communication, and mistrust. Put all three of these ideas into a sentence, which some call the central idea or the thesis:

> *The three leading causes of divorce are financial problems, lack of communication, and mistrust.*

The thesis will be the focal point of the essay and will allow your and readers to realize the direction your topic is going to take. For instance, at meetings agendas are provided, so the contents of the meeting are obvious to the attendees. Similarly, the thesis is the agenda of your essay.

Follow these guidelines for creating your thesis and you will find that with practice the creation of a central idea becomes easy, and once you have mastered the art you can experiment with your thesis.

1. As stated earlier, provide three main points in the thesis. You might ask why three? The reason is very simple, so you can write the five-paragraph essay with each main point becoming the three body paragraphs. The other two make up the introduction and conclusion. Moreover, psychologists tell us that we remember in multiples of three.

2. It is essential that as a beginning writer you construct your thesis as one sentence in which you include all three of the main ideas.

3. Make your thesis the last sentence of the introductory paragraph. This will allow you and your readers to see the connection of your main ideas of your body paragraphs to the thesis.

Outline

The next useful tool in the prewriting process is the outline. After the thesis is shaped, make an outline. In fact, the outline is a plan of the essay. Would you have your house built without a blueprint? That is highly unlikely. Without one, the builder might build a bathroom in the middle of your kitchen. Most would not appreciate that. Outlines are the blueprints of your essays, allowing you to keep your essay within the framework of your topic and assigned length. Most importantly, you can keep an eye on the thesis, main ideas, sub-ideas, and conclusion while you pen your composition. Supporting the main ideas and sub-ideas with evidence, facts, data, statistics, testimony, examples, and anecdotes make the writing process easy. It is almost like plugging these things and expanding the essay to its finale.

Outlines come in two forms, informal—also known as scratch outline—and formal. In informal outlines, you would just jot down the thesis, the main ideas, sub-ideas (if necessary sub sub-ideas—even sub, sub sub-ideas), and the conclusion. Unlike formal outlines, scratch outlines are not numbered and are similar to creating a list. However, working with formal outlines will enable you to become a better writer because they provide you with more organizational structure with your writing. Most accomplished writers use formal outlines. Below is a sample of a formal outline, which has been developed from the causes of divorce topic.

Causes of Divorce

Thesis: The three leading causes of divorce are financial problems, lack of communication, and mistrust.

I. *The first major reason for divorce is financial problems.*

   A.

   B.

II. *The second major reason for divorce is lack of communication.*

   A.

   B.

III. The final major reason for divorce is mistrust.

> *A.*

> *B.*

Conclusion:

For a myriad of causes married couples go their separate ways. Most divorces take place when couples face serious financial troubles. Others decide to divorce when they are unable to discuss and solve their marital problems. The other chief cause of the break up of marriages is when doubt sets in one or both of the spouses. Divorce rates will keep on climbing as couples look upon marriage as a disposable entity and new and more bizarre reasons will crop up.

These guidelines will help you formulate your outline:

1. On a blank sheet of paper, centering it, put the title of your essay. (See the above example.)

2. Next, key the word "thesis," followed by a colon and write your entire thesis as a complete sentence. (See the above example.)

3. Set the three main ideas of the body paragraphs with capital Roman numerals, followed by periods, for example I., II., and III. (See the above example.)

4. Word process sub-ideas with upper case letters, followed by periods, such as A., and B. (See the above example.) Sub-ideas must be divided into at least two parts, such as A or B. If you have more than two sub-ideas, you need to have C., D., and so on.

5. If you have sub-ideas of sub-ideas, you need to use Arabic numerals, such as 1. and 2. Furthermore, for more sub-ideas use lower case alphabets and lower case Roman numerals. Below is an example of the system of using alphabets and numbers for sub-ideas and their sub-ideas.

I.

    A.

       1.

       2.

    B.

II.

    A.

    B.

       1.

       2.

          a.

          b.

             i.

             ii.

III.

    A.

    B.

6.   Remember, an outline is just a plan. Therefore, it can be modified as better thoughts enter your mind.

2

Writing

hen you have followed the steps of the prewriting stage, you are ready to begin writing your essay—the first draft, of course. This is when the fingers meet the keyboard, or the pen meets the paper. Be sure in finishing your chores, putting the children to bed, making your phone calls, and completing whatever else you do that is distracting. If you like music, put on your favorite tunes. Watching television, while composing your essay, however, is not a good idea. A word of caution, an essay written at midnight before it is due will most likely have several problems. Pacing your assignment over a number of days will help you do a better job.

Paragraphs

Usually the five-paragraph essay is 500 to 750 words long. You might even be assigned a composition that is 1000 words long. That does not mean every paragraph is going to be neatly divided into 100, 150, or 200 words. Some paragraphs are going to be longer than others. A word of caution, a paragraph cannot be shorter that three sentences. The following diagram of a paragraph will help you understand this concept.

The first sentence of the paragraph acts as the topic sentence.

The second sentence of the paragraph acts as the supporting sentence.

The third sentence of the paragraph acts as the concluding sentence or a transitional sentence for the next paragraph—if there is one.

Be aware in writing a paragraph that is too long. A paragraph of more than 250 words (a double-spaced word- processed page) is the limit. Longer paragraphs bore the readers. Simply put, readers lack patience. A topic sentence is similar to the thesis statement. The topic sentence is a one-sentence summation of the paragraph, as a thesis is for the entire essay. The concluding sentence of a paragraph puts a wrap on the paragraph. On the other hand, the last sentence that is used as a transitional one works to bridge on to the next paragraph—providing unity to the composition. Usually, a three-sentence paragraph serves as a transitional paragraph.

The Introduction

The first or introductory paragraph has to be well crafted for the readers to be interested in the rest of the essay. Consequently, care must be taken. Serving as an attention getter, the first sentence leads readers into the essay. There are a number of tactics that can be used to write the attention getter. Some of the most widely used ones are listed below.

1. Start by asking a question. For example, "Do you know that 60 percent of the marriages end up in divorce"?

2. Start by using statistics. For example, "Sixty percent of the marriages end in divorce." Many like statistics because it provides solid evidence. Others find problems with it because it can be bent to suit the needs of vested interests.

3. Besides, statistics must be supported with their sources. Sources will lend credibility to the statistics.

4.   Start by using a bold statement. For example, "Marriage as an institution should be abolished since 60 percent of it end in divorce."

5.   Start by using an anecdote (story). For example, "Last June I was the best man at my friend's wedding. Following the ceremony, the couple went off on their honeymoon and to make a life themselves. The next time I saw my friend was at a New Year's Eve party, where I inquired about his bride. My friend replied that they were no longer together. That is the status of marriage. Sixty percent of marriages do not last. ...."

6.   Start by using a quotation. For example, "My best friend says, 'Marriage sucks.' She ought to know since she has been married thrice and divorced thrice. Sixty percent of marriages end in divorce. ...." You can also find quotations, spoken by famous people, on any topic. *Bartlett's Familiar Quotations. The 2,548 Best Things Anybody Ever Said, 21st Century Dictionary of Quotations,* and *Collection of Familiar Quotations* can provide you with quotations of prominent people.

7.   Start by using humor. A good joke can serve as a great attention getter. This tactic can backfire. If you tell a joke and none of friends laugh, it is a good idea to avoid this device.

The Body

   For the five-paragraph essay, the body consists of three paragraphs—developed from the three main ideas of your outline. These three paragraphs need to be expanded with the use of the sub-ideas also listed from each of your main ideas in the outline. Supporting ideas come from a number of sources. They include examples, statistics, testimony, and anecdotes. Main ideas are the skeleton of the essay, and the meat comes from the above sources which will shape the body. Think about these two examples. A man is charged with murder. His attorney gets up and tells the jury: "Ladies and gentleman of the jury, my client is not guilty. I rest my case. Another man is charged with murder, too. His lawyer tells the jury: "Ladies and gentleman of the jury, my client is not guilty of the charges leveled against him. I will prove to you that he was not even in Atlanta when the murder took place. He has in New York City, sitting at a bar. The bartender and several patrons of the pub will testify to that fact. They remember my client because he had asked for a Heineken Beer, but the barkeeper gave him a bottle of Miller beer. Upset, my client threw the beer back at him, missing him narrowly." Of the two lawyers, the second one is obviously much better for having provided more evidence. Accordingly, good development is essential.

Organizational Patterns

Development must follow an organizational pattern. A well organized essay is easy to read and raises the credibility of the writer for being methodical and not unorganized.

There are three ways of organizing your composition.

Chronological Order

Chronology comes from the Greek word chronos, meaning unfolding in a time sequence. You can start a story at the beginning then travel until it ends logically, or it can begin at the end and finish at the beginning. For example, a historical account usually commences at the onset of the event and stops when it is over.

Spatial Order

This type of organization is used in describing people, places, and things. In describing a room, begin from the left or the right and come to the starting point or from the right to the left. You can also begin from the ceiling to the floor or from the floor to the ceiling. For a person, you can begin describing from the head to the toes or from the toes to the head. The point of this order is not to jump around. For example, you describe a person's face first, then his stomach, next his hands and so on. This description will be confusing to the readers.

Logical Order

Some ideas need to be put in a logical order. The English alphabet follows the sequence of A, B, C and so on. For numbers, one comes before two, two before three, and so on.

Transitions

Good writing reads well and moves smoothly from paragraph to paragraph (and sentence to sentence.) The key is the use of transitions. Transitions logically connect ideas and exhibit shift from one idea to another, bringing about coherence. In the opinion of many scholars, transitions are hallmarks of good writing, so learn to use them. Below is a list of transitions.

(Addition): in addition, besides, moreover, further, furthermore, too, first, second, next, incidentally, by the way, too, in the first place, in the second place, last, lastly, finally, as well

(Comparison): similarly, also, likewise, in the same way, in the same manner, whereas

(Contrast): however, nevertheless, nonetheless, in contrast, still, on the other hand, still, anyway, actually, in reality, at any rate, at the same time, all the same, by contrast, on the contrary, otherwise, actually

(Result): therefore, thus, so, as a result, hence, after all, in fact, as a matter of fact, by this means, accordingly, consequently, naturally, of course, with this end, to this end, because of this, to this end, with this end, because of this, in any case, in conclusion

(Example): for example, for instance, such as, in fact, specifically, in particular, instead, in other words, in fact, that is, in brief, in conclusion, to summarize

(Time): after, later, since, as, before, next, immediately, then, later, eventually, at the same time, today, nowadays, then, when, while, in the beginning, to begin, in the meantime, in the future, finally,

(Direction): here, there, nearby, above, below, further on, behind, opposite, on the opposite side, close, on the right, on the left

Sentences

Sentences are the building blocks of paragraphs. Through the understanding of the structure of sentences, you can fashion better sentences. A sentence has to have a subject and a verb. The subject is either a noun or a pronoun and is the one which performs the action of the sentence. A clause can be either independent or dependent. An independent clause includes a subject and a verb and can stand alone as a complete sentence. Despite containing a subject and a verb, a dependent clause cannot stand alone. In order to be a complete sentence, the dependent clause needs to be attached to an independent clause. Sentences are categorized as simple, compound, complex, and compound-complex.

Simple sentence

A simple sentence has a subject and a verb and acts as one independent clause, as in this example:

Mallory walks to school everyday.
subject (Mallory)   verb (walks)

Compound sentence

A compound sentence has two independent clauses joined by a comma and a coordinating conjunction (see the list of coordinating conjunctions in the Errors List), as in this example

Tom walks to school, and his brother drives to work.

subject (Tom)   conjunction (and)

subject (his brother)   verb (walks)   verb (drives)

Complex sentence

A complex sentence has one independent clause and one or more dependent clauses. For example:

Because it has rained everyday of the month, the grass has grown faster than usual.

dependent clause (Because it has rained everyday of the month)
independent clause (the grass has grown faster than usual)

Compound-complex sentence

A compound-complex sentence has two or more independent clauses and one or more dependent clauses. For example:

Tom went to school, and his brother went to the doctor because he was sick.

independent clause (Tom went to school)
independent clause (his brother went to the doctor)
dependent clause (because he was sick)

A final word about sentences

The trick to becoming a skilled writer is remembering the KISS (Keep It Simple Stupid) principle. That means the use of simple and compound sentences with transitions. Your composition will be easy to read. Of course, the inclusion of a complex and a compound-complex sentence now and then will flavor your essay. Remember, the more complicated your writing is the chances of making mistakes are greater. Think about books that are easy to comprehend. They are not written in a complicated manner.

Words

Likewise, the KISS principle applies to your choice of words. Stay away from "big" or overly fancy words. When your readers fumble through the pages of a dictionary to understand what you are trying to saying, your writing will prove to be distracting. For example: The *outdoor repast* was *repositioned* to the indoors due to heavy *precipitation*.

The same sentence can be written by substituting "outdoor repast" with picnic, "repositioned" with moved, and "precipitation" with rain.

Also, steer clear of wordiness. The above sentence can be rewritten, thus: The picnic was moved indoors because of heavy rains. Not only have the uncommon words have been replaced, the sentence is more precise—losing its wordiness. Do not say something in seven words when you can say it in five.

Readers prefer concrete words over abstract words. Concrete words signify physical objects or terms that are related to the five senses. For example: motorcycle, sandwich, geranium. Abstract words, by contrast, are ones that ideas, feelings, and emotions. For example: love, justice, concept, cute. Concrete words draw pictures in the minds of your readers. By contrast, abstract words fail to paint mental pictures or evoke the senses. As a result, precision in writing can only be achieved through the use of vivid and precise words, although abstract words sometimes have a role in writing.

Inclusive Language

Language is a powerful tool, and, thus, needs to be used responsibly. People's sensibilities can be hurt; therefore, avoid stereotyping, demeaning, or patronizing language on the basis of race, ethnicity, gender, sexual orientation, political affiliation, disability and other reasons. If you are unsure about a classification, seek guidance. Nevertheless, the following principles will help you.

1. Avoid the generic *he*. In the past, *he*, *him*, and *his* were used to indicate people of either gender. The correct thing is to use *his or her, him or her,* and *his and her.* For a few times this form is fine, but it gets tiring very soon. To get around from your essay becoming boring, use plural subjects. For example: A professor takes *his or her* grading seriously. A much improved example: Professors take *their* grading seriously.

2. Avoid the generic *man* in referring to both men and women—also as a suffix for many professions. This is also an old term. One way is to drop the suffix, and the other is to learn the new the designations. Some of them are:

Incorrect	Correct
fireman	firefighter
policeman	police officer
mailman	mailperson, mail carrier, postal carrier
garbage man/trash man	garbage/trash collector
mankind	humans, people
to man (verb)	staff, operate
chairman	chairperson,, chair, head
businessman	businessperson, entrepreneur
salesman	salesperson, sales representative

4. Avoid using terms that are racially and ethnically stereotypical. In other words, it is wrong to label people. Below are some correct and incorrect terms.

Incorrect	Correct
Oriental (to be used for furniture and other items)	Asian (to be used for all Asians, including Japanese, Chinese, Laotians, Indians, Bangladeshis, and others)
Mexican, Puerto Rican, and others from Latin and South America	Latino (not Hispanic)
Red Indian	Native Americans (Tribal names are preferable if they are known.)

5. Avoid personal traits that are unrelated to the topic. For instance:
Colin Powell, an African-American man, served as President George Bush's first secretary of state.
Walter, a Chinese immigrant, donated blood.

6. Avoid other expressions, such as calling *disabled* people *crippled* which is a term of ridicule and disparagement. Calling someone *handicapped* is also derisive because it portrays the disabled as those who hold out their caps to beg for money. *Homosexuals* like to be called gays and lesbians or just gays or lesbians, appropriate to their sexual orientation.

The Conclusion

When you are formulating your essay, you need to compose your conclusion which can be incorporated into your essay as the fifth paragraph. The conclusion provides a closure for the essay which you have diligently written. Although the conclusion reiterates the introduction, it has to add something new to it so the essay ends in a memorable manner. Reminiscent of the introduction, a good conclusion employs a number of strategies:

1. You can ask a question.

2. You can use a quotation.

3. You can use an anecdote.

4. You can offer solutions for problems you might have posed.

5. You can use humor. (Again, use this strategy sparingly.)

6. You can restate an idea that you might have brought up at the beginning of the essay.

A word of caution though, the conclusion should be lively and thought provoking.

Under no circumstance should the conclusion offer apologies. Some do that which leaves the readers to question the writer's competence.

Diagram of an Essay

An essay has the following parts: introduction, body, and conclusion.

Introduction

Attention getter

Supporting ideas

Thesis

Body

I. Main idea

   A.   Sub-idea

   B.   Sub-idea

II. Main idea

   A.   Sub-idea

   B.   Sub-idea

III. Main idea

   A.   Sub-idea

   B.   Sub-idea

Conclusion

Types of Essays (Organizational Patterns)

In a college composition course, you will be asked to write several types of essays. Although they are individual patterns, they can merge together. In a narration, for example, you will find a lot of description. Below are the common kinds of essays

1. Narration tells a story. Good story telling is innate in every human being. People like to hear and read stories. People are even persuaded with stories.

2. Description uses the five senses of sight, smell, touch, taste, and sound. Using these elements can heighten the depiction of a person, place, or thing.

3. Definition delineates a term without making the dictionary meaning as the centerpiece of the writing. Instead, the writing will use examples, classifications, characterizations, and other means.

4. Process is a technique in which an explanation is given of how something works or is done.

5. Comparison and contrast is an organizational pattern that lists the similarities and differences. An essay, using this pattern, can be written in the normal five-paragraph format or the four-paragraph format. The four-paragraph arrangement is only to be used with the comparison and contrast model. In the five-paragraph comparison and contrast writing, each of the three body paragraphs will constitute of one similarity, followed by a difference. Conversely, the four-paragraph essay will contain all of the similarities in one paragraph and all the other differences in the next one, topped off by the introduction and conclusion.

6. Classification/division catalogs different ideas under one category. For instance, in the first paragraph (introductory) introduce the classification/division topic. Then, in each of the three body paragraphs, provide a part of the topic in a parallel form.

7. Cause and effect is another way writing can be organized or from effect to cause. You can start by recording the cause and then listing the effects. On the other hand, you can provide the effect first and follow it up with the causes.

8. Examples are the last type of organizing an essay. Here, you will begin by making a general statement of the topic in the introductory paragraph. Follow it up with three body paragraphs, each one with one or more examples.

3

Rewriting

ou are almost there. If you are at the rewriting stage, you have completed the two of the three most difficult aspects of the writing process. Now diligently follow the rewriting steps (revising, editing, and proofreading) in order to produce an essay that will make you proud and earn you a decent grade. The first draft is far from a completed essay. Those who call themselves writers toil through several drafts to come up with a final product. Leo Tolstoy, the famous Russian novelist, avoided looking at his published works because he wanted to revise them. The Irish writer Oscar Wilde once said that it took him all morning to put in a comma, and it took him all afternoon to take it out. Those two authors are somewhat extreme cases.

Nevertheless, you should finish your essay ahead of time so you can revise, edit, and proofread it. When you finish your composition and start the rewriting process at a later time, perhaps a day or two later, you will be surprised how easily you can catch your own errors. By catching your own mistakes, you can help from losing points. Reading your composition out loud is another way of catching your own mistakes because hearing what you wrote allows you to discern what your readers are reading.

21

Revision

Revision is the first step. In this stage, you undertake major changes to your writing. Cut out paragraphs that lack focus or stray from the topic. Move paragraphs around, so they transition well from one idea to another. You might say, "Well, I followed my outline. Then, why should I stray from it"? The outline is not permanent and is just a plan. If new inspirations make more sense, by all means make the changes. In other words, you perform major surgery to your composition in this phase. When revising, you should pay attention to content and organization.

Content

1. Does your essay meet the assigned length?

2. Does your essay have adequate controlling ideas?

3. Does your essay have enough examples and illustrations?

4. Does your essay address topics?

Organization

1. Does your essay have well developed paragraphs?

2. Does your essay have unity?

3. Does your essay have coherence?

4. Does your essay follow the organizational pattern you have chosen?

Answer the above questions, and make your corrections as you proceed. Do not be afraid of marking your paper up. It is much better for you to color it red, rather than the instructor doing so. Some instructors require the inclusion of your first and however many drafts you go through with your final version of the essay. These instructors are looking to see if you went through your work and are learning revising, editing, and proofreading skills.

Editing

Now comes the nitty gritty part of the rewriting process. In the editing step, attention is paid to grammar, punctuation, and mechanics—making your focus narrower. Similar to the revising step, let your essay sit for a little while. Read your essay out aloud, as you did while revising, so you can hear the sentences to see if they make sense and they flow well. By being mindful of the following items, you will make editing more efficient.

Mechanics and Grammar

1. Have you avoided fragments?

2. Have you avoided comma splices?

3. Have you avoided run-on sentences?

4. Do your subjects and verbs agree?

5. Do your pronouns agree with their antecedents?

6. Do you have your verbs in the proper tense in keeping with the tone of the essay?

7. Have you checked for misspelled words?

8. Have you checked the punctuation?

9. Have you avoided wordiness?

10. Have you used appropriate capitalization?

11. Have you avoided colloquialisms, slangs, clichés, and jargons?

A review of grammar, punctuation, and mechanics has been presented in Section V of this book.

Proof reading

You have done everything prescribed in this book, and you feel your essay is ready for submission. You are feeling good. Just one final thing: Go over the composition one more time. This time, it is to proofread it which is checking for missing words, punctuation, page numbers, and the like. You might have word processed the same word twice. In this case the word book is mistakenly put in twice: Alaina borrowed three *books books* on American history. Additionally, check for irregular spacing. In this step, too, the prescription is to read each word out loudly, enabling you to do a better job at reducing unwanted errors.

4

Plagiarism

Plagiarism is a dirty word in academia. Appropriating other people's writing and passing it off as your own is considered to be a major offence. It is considered academic stealing. The difference between going to a parking lot and prying off someone else's hubcaps stealing intellectual property is the same. Some feel that anything can be taken from the Internet and incorporated into papers and other documents. Internet sources have to be documented, too. Those websites you visited could also be accessed by your professors. To safeguard yourself from charges of plagiarism, simply document your sources. Otherwise, the consequences are pretty serious. Some universities and colleges will haul you before a disciplinary board; others will fail you in the course; still others will give you a failing grade for the writing, which contains plagiarized material. The advice is a resounding: Do not the do it. It is not worth it.

5

Problem Areas: Grammar, Punctuation, Mechanics, and Other Ways to Correct Them

This section highlights grammatical, mechanical, and spelling errors which are widespread in college composition. Along with drawing attention to them, you will get a quick review of the problem areas so you can learn the rules to gain competence in your writing.

Subject-verb Agreement (s/v agr)

Subjects must agree with their verbs (sometimes also called predicates). In order for that to happen, you must keep in mind several rules:

1. Singular subjects take singular verbs; plural subjects take plural subjects.

Tom drives to work everyday. Singular subject = Tom; singular verb = drives.

Cats chase mice. Plural subject = cats; plural verb = chase

2. Prepositional phrases can come between the subject and verb. In that case, overlook the prepositional phrase and make the subject agree with the verb.

One of my best friends is a lawyer. Prepositional phrase = of my best friends; singular subject = one; singular verb = is.

3. Two subjects, joined to each other by and, is considered a plural subject, which will naturally take a plural verb.

Jay Leno and Conan O'Brien are two late night comedians on NBC.

Plural subject = Jay Leno and Conan O'Brien; plural verb = are

When the compound subject forms a single idea, use a singular verb.

Speech and theatre is the name of a college department.

Singular subject = speech theatre; singular verb = is

4. When subjects are separated by or or nor (or by either and neither), the subject nearest the verb need to agree.

My brother or my parents are going to represent me at the meeting.

Plural subject = parents; plural verb = are

My parents or my brother is going to represent me at the meeting.

Singular subject = brother, singular verb = is

Neither the boys nor their father is going to meet the principal.

Singular subject = father; singular verb: is

5. Indefinite pronouns, as subjects, always take singular verbs. These are indefinite pronouns:

each	anyone	anybody	anything
either	everyone	everybody	everything
neither	someone	somebody	something
one	no one	nobody	nothing

An example of a sentence with an indefinite pronoun follows: Nobody is at home.

Singular subject = nobody, singular verb = is

6. Collective nouns, as subjects, take singular verbs. Some collective nouns are words board of trustees, team, jury, faculty, committee, family, couple, crowd, and audience. The faculty meets this Friday in the conference room. Singular subject = faculty; singular verb: meets

7. Subjects that seem to be plurals with an s at the end, although singular in meaning, take on a singular verb. Examples of such words are news, statistics, economics, athletics, mathematics, politics, and physics.

    Mathematics is one of the most difficult subjects for college students.

8. When verbs come before the subjects, the subjects must take the appropriate verbs. Usually, in a sentence the verb follows the subject. However, in some, the verbs precede the subject.
    Here is the book you are supposed to read for the class.
    Singular verb = is; singular subject = book
    There were ten people at my party.
    Plural verb = were; plural subject = people

9. Gerunds, and titles of books, films, and company names will always take singular verbs. Gerund phrases are verbs ending in ing and followed by modifiers, complements, or objects.
    Answering the phone is the job of the intern.
    Gerund: answering the phone; singular verb= is
    Proctor and Gamble manufactures many of our household products.
    Title of company = Proctor and Gamble; singular verb = manufactures

Verbs (*verb, vt*)

Verbs give many beginning writers problems. Common verb problems involve *be* verbs, regular and irregular verbs, verb tense shifts, and standard and nonstandard verbs.

Be Verbs

Be verbs (*is, am, was, were, been, being*) are troublesome. It is not uncommon to hear, even sometimes read in college essays, the *be* verb in this manner: I be at my mother's house when the child knocked at the door. Despite this incorrect use of *be* verb, they make sentences tedious and uninteresting. The ways to correct them involve using action verbs, changing passive voice to active voice (See voice in this Section.), changing nominalizations (See nominalizations in this chapter.) to verbs, and combining sentences to form compound ones.

(Weak form of the *be* verb):   The television network is planning to broadcast five new reality shows this fall.

(Better form of the *be* verb):   The televisions network plans to broadcast five new reality shows this fall.

Helping Verbs

On many occasions, verbs perform their actions with some help from other verbs. Common helping verbs are *is, are, was, are, were, will, be, have, has, had, do, does, did, can, could, may might, must, shall, should,* and *could.* They come before the main verbs. The helping the helping verb and the main together are known as verbal phrases.

Regular and Irregular Verbs

Verbs can be either regular or irregular. Most verbs in the English language are regular. These regular verbs have four principal parts: present, past, future, past participle, and present participle. For example,

Present	Past	Past Participle	Present Participle
talk	talked	talked	talking
call	called	called	calling
cause	caused	caused	causing

Two things should be noted about regular verbs.

1. Past tense and past participles are formed by adding *d* or *ed* the present tense form of the verb. Talk becomes talked in the past and past participle forms.

2. Past participle forms have to employ helping verbs, such as has, have, or had or is, are, was, or were. For example: Jane has talked to me about her plans to attend a private university.

Irregular verbs can be confusing since the majority of them change their spellings in the past and past participle forms. Some of them keep the same spelling in the past and past participle forms as in the present tense. Nonetheless, the present participle is formed in the same way as is done in regular verbs by adding *ing*. The following is a list of common irregular verbs that can be useful.

Present	Past	Past Participle	Present Participle
be	was, were	been	being
beat	beaten	beaten, beat	being
become	became	become	becoming
begin	began	begun	beginning

bite	bit	bitten, bit	biting
blow	blew	blown	blowing
break	broke	broken	breaking
bring	brought	brought	bringing
burst	burst	burst	bursting
buy	bought	bought	buying
catch	caught	caught	catching
choose	chose	chosen	choosing
come	came	come	coming
cost	cost	cost	costing
cut	cut	cut	cutting
deal	dealt	dealt	dealing
dig	dug	dug	digging
dived	dived dove	dived	diving
do	did	done	doing
draw	drew	drawn	drawing
eat	ate	eaten	eating
fall	fell	fallen	falling
feel	felt	fallen	feeling
find	found	found	finding
fight	fought	fought	fighting

fly	flew	flown	flying
freeze	froze	frozen	freezing
get	got	got, gotten	getting
give	gave	given	giving
go	gone	went	going
grow	grew	grown	growing
hang	hung	hung	hanging
have	had	had	having
hear	heard	heard	hearing
hide	hid	hidden	hiding
hit	hit	hit	hitting
hurt	hurt	hurt	hurting
keep	kept	kept	keeping
know	knew	known	knowing
lay	laid	laid	laying
lead	led	led	leading
lend	lent	lent	lending
lie	lay	lain	lying
lose	lost	lost	losing
make	made	made	making
mean	meant	meant	meaning

pay	paid	paid	paying
prove	proved	proved proven	proving
read	read	read	reading
ride	rode	ridden	riding
rise	rose	risen	rising
run	ran	run	running
say	said	said	saying
see	saw	seen	seeing
send	sent	sent	sending
set	set	set	setting
sell	sold	sold	selling
shake	shook	shaken	shaking
show	showed	showed shown	showing
shoot	shot	shot	shooting
shrink	shrank	shrunk	shrinking
sing	sang	sung	singing
sink	sank	sunk	sinking
sit	sat	sat	sitting
sleep	slept	slept	sleeping
speak	spoke	spoken	speaking

spin	spun	spun	spinning
sell	sold	sold	selling
stand	stood	stood	standing
steal	stole	stolen	stealing
stick	stuck	stuck	sticking
sting	stung	stung	stinging
strike	struck	struck stricken	striking
swear	swore	sworn	swearing
swim	swam	swum	swimming
take	took	taken	taking
teach	taught	taught	teaching
tell	told	told	telling
think	thought	thought	thinking
throw	threw	thrown	throwing
wake	woke waked	woken waked	waking
wear	wore	worn	wearing
win	won	won	winning
wring	wrung	wrung	wining
write	wrote	written	written

Sentence Fragments (frag)

A sentence fragment lacks the ingredients of a sentence, such as a subject, a complete verb, or making complete sense. Examples of fragments are as follows:

Talking on the phone.
Paper plates and cups strewn all over the lawn.
Although I am contented with my job.

Subject

In order to correct fragments, the first thing to do is ask the question: Does the statement have a subject? If one is missing, adding a subject can turn the fragment into a sentence.

Picked up milk from the grocery. (*Who did?)*
By adding the subject *John*, the statement will be a complete one:
John picked up milk from the grocery.

Complete Predicate

Another question, you should ask: Does the statement have a complete verb?

She talking on the phone.

The verb is incomplete. By adding the helping verb *is*, the statement becomes complete.

She is talking on the phone.

Another thing that can create a fragment is the use of *ing* or *to* verb at the beginning or end of a sentence.

Milton was sick. Fighting a virus for a week.

The second statement is a fragment, which can be corrected by replacing the period with a comma after *sick* and making *a* of *appearing* into a lower case.

Milton was sick, fighting a virus for a week

Dependent Words

Another way to test for fragments is to ask the question: Are statements with dependent words connected to complete sentences (independent clauses)? Dependent clauses have subject and verbs, but they begin with subordinating conjunctions (such as if, because, or when) or relative pronouns (such as who, which, or that).

Because her opposition to the city dump is well known.

That you drove this morning.

Dependent-word statements can be corrected by connecting them to complete sentences or rewriting them.

(Attached to a sentence):	Because her opposition to the city dump is well known, she is respected by those in the environmental movement.
(Correct):	Her opposition to the city dump has made her respected in the environmental movement.
(Attached to a sentence):	Marcus has an antique car that you drove this morning.
(Correct):	You drove Marcus' antique car this morning.

In order for you to recognize dependent words, a list of the common words is given below.

after	if	what
although	since	when
because	that	which
before	unless	while
even if	until	who

Comma splice (*cs*)

A comma splice occurs when two sentences (independent clauses) are joined by a comma. For instance: Mighty Mouse has been absent from movie screens for a number of years, Mickey Mouse is doing well in Disney's theme parks. Commas are not strong enough to bridge the sentences. There are ways by which comma splices can be corrected.

Using Coordinating Conjunctions

A statement with a comma splice can be fixed by inserting a coordinating conjunction after the comma between the two sentences. (See discussion of coordinating conjunctions in this chapter.) For example: Mighty Mouse had been absent from movie screens for a number of years, but Mickey Mouse is doing well in Disney's theme parks. Here the coordinating conjunction *but* has been put behind the comma, separating the two sentences.

Using Semicolons

Another method of correcting a comma splice is by replacing the comma with a semicolon, as in this example: Mighty Mouse has been absent from movie screens for a number of years; Mickey Mouse is doing well in Disney's theme parks. In this instance, the comma was replaced with a semicolon.

Using Dependent Words

The three methods is to replace the comma in the statement with a dependent word. (See the list of common dependent words in this Section.) For example: Mighty Mouse has been absent from movie screens for a number of years while Mickey Mouse is doing well in Disney's theme parks.

Breaking into Two Sentences

The final way to correct a comma splice is by replacing the comma between the two sentences and making them into two separate ones. Further, the first letter of the first word needs to be rewritten in the upper case.

For example: Mighty Mouse has been absent from movie screens for a number of years, Mickey Mouse is doing well in Disney's theme parks.

For example: Mighty Mouse has been absent from movie screens for a number of years. Mickey Mouse is doing well in Disney's theme parks.

Note that a complete sentence followed by the second, which is preceded by a transition (see in chapter on writing), can become a comma splice if a comma comes before the transition. The problem can be fixed by replacing the comma with a semicolon or break it up into two separate sentences.

Run-ons (ro)

When two sentences are joined together without any punctuation between the two, that statement is known as a run-on sentence. Some instructors also call it a fused sentence (fs). An example of a run-on follows: College students go to bed late they avoid early morning classes. There are three ways of fixing run-on sentences.

Breaking into Two Sentences

Run-ons can be corrected by separating the two sentences. Further, the first letter of the first word needs to be rewritten in the upper case.

College students go to bed late they avoid early morning classes.

College students go to bed late. They avoid early morning classes.

Using Commas and Coordinating Conjunctions

To fix a run-on, put a comma and a coordinating conjunction after it. (See in this chapter a list of coordinating conjunctions.)

College students go to bed late they avoid early morning classes.

College students go to bed late, so they avoid early morning classes

Here the coordinating conjunction *so* was used after inserting a comma between the two sentences.

Using Dependent Words

The third method is through the use of dependent words. (See the list of common dependent words in this chapter.)

College students go to bed late they avoid early morning classes.

Because college students go to bed late, they avoid early morning classes

Nonetheless, remember that a comma goes at the end of the dependent clause before the independent clause.

Using Semicolons

The last method of correcting a run-on is by inserting a semicolon between the two sentences (independent clauses).

College students go to bed late they avoid early morning classes.

College students go to bed late; they avoid early morning classes.

Pronoun references (ref)

If you keep using nouns over and over again, writing becomes tedious so refrain from using them. Pronouns are substitute for nouns. There are two types of pronouns: personal and indefinite pronouns. Personal pronouns are *I, me, my, mine, you, yours, he, him, his, she, her, hers, it, its, we, our, ours, they, them, their, theirs.* The following is a list of indefinite pronouns.

each	anyone	anybody	anything
either	everyone	everybody	everything
neither	someone	somebody	something
one	on one	nobody	nothing

Pronouns are tricky. They must agree to their antecedents. Otherwise, you have a pronoun reference error. Overall, pronouns can give many problems but if you take care, you can avoid problems with them.

Agreement in Number and Gender

A pronoun must agree in number and gender to its antecedent. Singular nouns will take singular pronouns; plural nouns will take plural pronouns.

Tasha found her car in the parking lot.

The pronoun *her* agrees with the noun Tasha in number (singular) and gender (female).

Indefinite Pronouns

Indefinite pronouns convey reference to unspecified people or objects. At first glance, indefinite pronouns appear to be plural in form although they are not. (Indefinite pronouns are listed above.).

Everybody has to drive *their* car
Everybody has to drive *his or her* car.
The *he* or *she* (*his* or her) construction is awkward, so rewrite the sentence with a plural subject and a plural personal pronoun.
A flight attendant takes his or her responsibility seriously during in-flight emergencies.

Flight attendants take their responsibilities seriously during in-flight emergencies.

They and You

On many occasions, reference is made to people or objects with the use of the generalized *they* or *you*. These words are vague.

(Vague):	They say that college athletes should receive stipends.
(More definite):	Some newspaper columnists say that college athletes should receive stipends.
(Vague):	You have to avoid road rage.
(More definite):	We have to avoid road rage.

Pronoun Shift

A pronoun shift takes place when the point of view is changed from one person to another. Below are the three pronoun points of view.

Persons

	First	*Second*	*Third*
Singular	I, me, my, mine	you, your	he, him, his
			she, her, it, its
Plural	we, us, our	you, your	they, them, their

We take a vacation every summer, and you will find Alaska has the most beautiful scenery. Here the second-person view point *you* shifts from the third-person point of view *we*.

We take a vacation every summer, and we found Alaska to have the most beautiful scenery. In this sentence both pronouns are in the same point of view *we*.

Reference to Multiple Antecedents

Problems occur when a pronoun refers to multiple nouns in a sentence.

Martha and Elizabeth are twins, but she is taller of the two. Who is taller? We are not sure.

Martha and Elizabeth are twins, but Martha is taller of the two. Now we know who is taller.

It, That, This, Which

These four pronouns are also troublesome. Sometimes when they are used in sentences, their reference is unclear.

I bought a watch, pen, and cell phone. It cost fifty dollars. What cost fifty dollars? We do not know.

I bought a watch, pen, and cell phone, and the phone cost fifty dollars.

The CD and the book are best sellers, but this is better. What is better? We are not sure.

The CD and the book are best sellers, but this book is better. Now, the pronoun *this* pulls in the reference *book*.

Collective Nouns

Collective nouns signify groups, such as *audience, class, committee, company, couple, crowd, family, group, jury, school,* and *team.* Thus, they need to take singular forms of pronouns, as in this example: The team lost its mascot.

Pronoun Case

You have heard people say, "Me and Tommy waded through the creek to reach safety;" or "Us four played volleyball during the summer;" or "The real estate agent handed the house key to Tabitha and he." These sentences are incorrect. The rule is to use subjective case when the pronoun is the subject of a sentence and to use the objective case when the pronoun is an object of the verb or preposition. The following are objective and subjective cases.

Subjective cases	*Objective cases*
I, you, he, she, it we, they, who, whoever	me, you, her, him, it, us, them, whom whomever

The above incorrect sentences can be thus corrected.

Tommy and I waded through the creek to reach safety. In this sentence, the pronoun *me* was replaced with the proper subjective case *I,* which was put after the subject Tommy. Always put yourself last when you have multiple subjects as a respect to the others.

We three played volleyball during the summer. The proper subjective case in this sentence is *we.*

The real estate agent handed the house key to Tabitha and he.

The real estate agent handed the house key to Tabitha and him. In this sentence, the objective case *him* was used instead of *he.*

Punctuation (p)

Proper punctuation provides readers the ability to pause. If not, they would be out of breath very soon. Placing a punctuation mark in its proper place takes some effort. Many students often complain that they have a hard time putting in commas.

End Punctuation

A period, question mark, and exclamation denote the end of a statement.

Period (.)

Periods are used to end a statement, a mild command, an indirect question, or most abbreviations, as shown in these examples.

Zinnias grow well in the summer heat.

Take the garbage to the curb.

Mirela asked if the house was on sale.

(Some abbreviations):   Mr., Mrs., Ms. Dr., B.A., M.A.,
                          Ph.D., a.m., p.m., Rd., St., e.g., i.e.

Avoid putting periods in acronyms, as these: USA, FBI, IRS, UNO, TN, USM, FDA, CDC, NAACP, NFL.

Question mark (?)

Question marks come at the end of direct question, as in this example: Did you eat breakfast?

Exclamation point (!)

Exclamation marks are used for indicating excitement or strong feeling. Using them too many times in your essay will prove ineffective. The trick is to just use a few for the dramatic effect, such as these:

Watch out for the motorcycle!

Happy birthday, Sarah!

Commas (,)

Commas, too, provide pause in sentences like end punctuations do. However, the pause is shorter than for periods, question marks, or exclamation marks. Commas give most people a fit, so learning how to use them will give you confidence with your writing.

In a series

Commas go between three items in a series, not between two, as in this case: The carpenter went to his work with his hammer, saw, and chisel.

Between Complete Thoughts (Separated by Coordinating Conjunctions)

When two sentences are joined together by a coordinating conjunction (see the section on coordinating conjunctions for a list of them), a comma is used to separate them. Place the comma in front of the coordinating conjunction, as in this example: Tom walks to school, but his brother drives to work.

After introductory material

After introductory words, phrases, and clauses, commas are needed, but short and unemphatic ones usually do not need them.

(Introductory word):	No, I am not interested buying a new car.
(Phrase):	Disappointed with his English grade, Milton decided to become a business major.
(Clause):	When it rains, the streets are flooded. (short and unemphatic): Yesterday she bought a computer.

Before and after Parenthetical Expressions

Put commas in front and behind parenthetical expressions.
Parenthetical expressions (also called nonrestrictive clauses) are
those words, phrases, or clauses that are not germane to the meaning
of the sentence. Avoid putting commas in either front or behind
restrictive clauses, which are important to the meaning of the
sentence. Examples are provided below.

(Nonrestrictive):	The boy, who lives in the red house, bought a scooter.
(Incorrect restrictive form):	Children enjoyed the cartoon movie, *Nemo*.
(Correct restrictive form):	Children enjoyed the cartoon movie *Nemo*.

With transitions

A comma comes after a transition when the transition is at the
beginning or end of a sentence. In the middle of a sentence, a
transition will take a comma in the front and back.

(At the beginning):	As a result, the marketing company is going to ake part in an opinion survey.
(At the end):	Fried chicken is full of saturated fat, for example.
(In the middle):	The graph, thus, is an example of the increase of prostrate cancer among African American males.

With direct quotations

Commas are used after direct quotations. Shorter quotations do
not take commas, as shown below.

Benjamin Franklin is purported to have said, "A penny saved is a
penny earned.

My mother has called me a "spendthrift" many times.

Between adjectives

When two or more adjectives modify the same noun, use commas to separate them. The rule is if you can separate the adjectives with *and,* put a comma, as in this instance: The sleek, black horse won two consecutive races.

With direct address

A comma or commas should be used with words of direct address. Examples are as follows:

(At the beginning, one comma):   Dr. Pavlov, please answer your phone.

(In the middle, two commas):   My job, Ms. Smith, is to check your blood pressure.

With titles, addresses, dates, and numbers

Examples of use of commas for titles, addresses, dates, and numbers are provided below,

(Title):   Michael Higgins, Ph.D., teaches American history to graduate students.

(Address):   Mrs. Lawrence mailed the package to 1203 Whispering Wood Road, Jackson, Tennessee 38305.

(Numbers):   1,000

                100,000

                1,000,000

Semicolons (;)

Semicolons fulfill two purposes in writing. First, they are used to separate a series which contains commas. Second, semicolons are used for joining two sentences (independent clauses) when the thoughts are closely related. Some examples of the use of semicolons are as follows.

(Incorrect use of semicolon in a series):	Dr. Wiggins has to attend meetings in Edison, New Jersey, Athens, Georgia, and Jackson, Mississippi.
(Correct use of semicolon in a series):	Dr. Wiggins has to attend meetings in Edison, New Jersey; Athens, Georgia; and Jackson, Mississippi.
(Joining two independent clauses):	The apple orchard belongs to Andy; he also has orange groves in Florida.

Colons (:)

Colons cause problems for some beginning writers in three different ways:

1. When a colon is placed after *to be* verbs,

2. When a colon is placed after prepositions, and

3. When a colon is placed after *for example, such as, or including.*

(Incorrect):	The ingredients of the cake are: flour, milk, eggs, pineapple chunks, sugar, and baking soda.
(Correct):	The ingredients of the cake are flour, milk, eggs, pineapple chunks, sugar, and baking soda.
(Incorrect):	The book consists of: ten chapters, appendices, and pictures.
(Correct):	The book consists of ten chapters, appendices, and pictures.

(Incorrect):   Many people worked on this project for example:
                      Anthony, Brian, and Jodie.

(Correct):   Many people worked on this project, for example
                      Anthony, Brian, and Jodie. Colons have the
                      following uses:

For a list

Colons are used for introducing a list.

These students are going on the field trip: Susan, Al, Trey,
Michele, and JoAnn.

For direct quotations

Colons are used to introduce long or literary quotations.

Frederick Douglass writes in his *Emancipation Proclaimed*:
"Common sense, the necessities of the war, to say nothing of the
dictation of justice and humanity have at last prevailed."

For a Final Summary or Explanation

Colons are used for introducing final summaries or explanations
to the first part of the sentence. Both parts must be complete
sentences (independent clauses).

The manager undertook the project with one goal: the project
will be completed on time.

For Salutations in a Formal Letter; Between Hours and Minutes;
Between Titles and Subtitles; Ratios; and Between City (State) and
Publisher in Reference Citations

Dear Mrs. Bradley

10:00 a.m. (A.M.)

3:1

The History of Tribal People: Maoris in New Zealand

Island Park, NY: Whittier

Apostrophes (')

Some are confused when to use the plural form of a noun or an apostrophe. Others are unsure how to use *it's* and *its*. *It's* is a contraction of it is, while *its* is a possessive pronoun.

(Incorrect):	The Yomamoto's live on top of the hill.
(Correct):	The Yomamotos live on top of the hill.
(Incorrect):	The University of Georgia has revised it's on-campus alcohol policy.
(Correct):	The University of Georgia has revised its on-campus alcohol policy.

Contractions

Apostrophes are used to form contractions. Contractions are good for conversations and informal writing, such as personal letters. Avoid contractions in formal writing.

> *I am* becomes *I'm*
> *she will* becomes *she'll*
> *does not* becomes *doesn't*
> *it is* becomes *it's*

Possessions

Apostrophes are used to show possession. The rule in this case is to add an *'s* to the singular noun that does not end in an *s*, also with the singular noun that ends in an *s*.

Some, on the other hand, avoid using the *'s* when the singular noun ends in an *s*. Both forms are acceptable.

Raja's bicycle was stolen.

Douglas's family is moving to California.
                        or
Douglas' family is moving to California.

For multiple nouns, apostrophes can be used in two ways—depending on the intended meaning:

1. If the nouns are used to indicate joint possession, the 's is added to the last noun.

    Tom and Jerry's antics have amused children for a long time.

2. If the nouns are used to emphasize separate possessions, the 's is added to each of the nouns.

    Aaron's and Jennifer's graduation parties are planned for the same day.

Plurals of Letters, Symbols, and Words as Words

Apostrophes are used to form plurals of letters, symbols, and words indicated as words.

Several students made A's in Dr. Fernandez's class.

She has too many #'s in her phone number.

Too many yes's will be looked upon with suspicion.

Hyphens (-)

When typing a hyphen, use one key stroke (-) to indicate this punctuation. Be sure to check the dictionary to make sure that the compound words require hyphens because some do not.

Division of compound words for describing a noun

Hyphens are used to join two or more words that describe a noun

The nine-year-old boy jumped over the fence. (Hyphens are used in-between *nine, year,* and *old* which describe the noun *boy.*)

The fish swim upstream through the quickly moving stream. (There is no hyphen between *quickly* and *stream* because *ly* adverbs describing a noun do not need one.)

Division of words at the end of lines

Hyphens can be used to divide words at the end of lines. However, the words can be divided only between syllables, and one-syllable words must never be divided. If you are in doubt, consult a dictionary.

Only 25 divers in her age group qual-
ified for the prestigious competition. (As an example, the word *qualified* has been divided with a hyphen between.)
Many experts believe that drinking te-
a cleanses the body of harmful chemicals. (T*ea* is a one-syllable word, so it cannot be divided.)

Division of fractions and numbers

Hyphens are used to indicate fractions and numbers from twenty-one and ninety-nine.

One-third of the class voted for having a pizza party at the end of the semester. (fraction)

When I arrived at the Social Security Office, twenty-five people were waiting ahead of me.

Dashes (—)

Typing two dashes without any space, in-between and before and after, will lengthen into a dash (—). Writers use dashes for several purposes.

Breaks in thought

Dashes are used to convey dramatic pause.

He kicked the ball into the net—making the winning goal.

Parenthetical expressions

Dashes are used to set off expressions that are more important to be enclosed within parentheses.

The member of the band—the one with the beard—has a master's degree from Harvard University.

Series which contain commas

Dashes are used in front and behind a series of nouns which contain commas.

The department's concentrations—journalism, public relations, and broadcasting—offer communication students a variety of choices for their majors.

Additional information after a sentence

Dashes are used for providing a list or an explanation for sentences.

The farmer had given his cows names—Bessie, Tessie, and Messie.

Parentheses ( )

Parentheses are used to enclose information less important within the sentence or more information, such as numbers.

The letter was mailed a week ago (August 5, 2003).

Tabitha took out a loan ($10,000) from the bank.

Brackets [ ]

Brackets are used to indicate writers' comments within direct quotations. The Latin word *sic* is put inside brackets to point out grammatical or spelling errors in direct quotations. The newspaper reported, "The museum [Smithsonian Institute] has a collection of vintage aircrafts.

A student wrote, "I am suppose [sic] to be in New York for my father's fiftieth birthday."

Ellipsis points (. . .)

Ellipsis points are used to indicate the omission of material from quotations. Three spaced periods indicate ellipsis points in the middle of quotations, four when the excluded material is at the end of the sentence.

(In the middle of a quotation): Charles Darwin writes "Every being ...must suffer destruction during some period of its life, and during the same season or occasional year,

otherwise, on the principle of geometrical increase, its numbers would quickly become so inordinately great that no country could support the product."

(At the end of the quotation): Mori Ogai writes, "The have finished loading the coal ....

Slashes (/)

Some use slashes for these forms: *and/or, he/she, his/her.* English professors frown upon such use for their awkwardness, yet slashes can come handy in your essay writing.

Separation of Quoted Lines of Poetry in a Sentence

Slashes are used to separate lines of quoted poetry which are put within a sentence. In this instance, each slash is preceded and followed by a single space.

Mirza Ghalib, the 19th century Indian poet, writes in "The drop dies in the river:" "The drop dies in the river/ of its joy/ pain goes so far it cures itself."

Indicating fractions

Slashes are used to indicate fractions in mathematics.

1/3   1/5   1/10

Quotation marks (") (')

Some common errors with quotation marks involve their use to draw attention to colloquialisms and slangs; indirect quotations, and around titles of your own essays.

(Incorrect):   He is always happy to see his "homeboys."

(Correct):   He is always happy to see his friends from his neighborhood.

(Incorrect):   Wanda said that "her life had taken a turn for the better."

(Correct):   Wanda said that her life had taken a turn for the better,

(Incorrect):   "The Definition of a Gentleman"

By

Ruth Sanders

Correct: The Definition of a Gentleman

By

Ruth Sanders

Quotation marks perform several functions in writing.

Set off Direct Quotations

Quotation marks are used to indicate material (words, phrases, sentences, and passages) directly borrowed from other sources. If the quotations are so long (over four lines), use the block form.

(Direct quotation):   In Goethe's *Faust*, Mephistopheles says, "O curses on this ninny band!"

(Block quotation) Rabindranath Tagore, the Nobel Prize winning author from India, describes one of his characters thus in "Broken Ties":

When I first met Satish he appeared to me like a constellation of stars, his eyes shining, his tapering fingers like flames of fire, his face glowing with a youthful radiance. I was surprised to find that most of his fellow students hated him, for no other fault than that he resembled himself more than he resembled others. Because with men, as well as with some insects, taking the colour of the surroundings is often the best means of self-protection.

Setting of Short Titles

Quotation marks are used to enclose the titles of newspaper and magazine articles, poems, short stories, chapters of books, songs, episodes of television and radio programs, and essays (not your own).

The class will discuss William Blake's "The Tyger."

Single Quotation Marks

Single quotation marks are used to enclose quotations inside quotations.

Peter Ivanovich announces the death of Tolstoy's protagonist in this manner: "'Gentleman,'" he said, "'Ivan Ilych has died.'"

Punctuation with Quotation Marks

The punctuation with quotation marks has to follow the established guidelines.

Commas and Periods

Commas and periods go inside punctuation marks.

"Mr. Perkins cannot be found guilty," his lawyer argued, "as he was locked up in the state penitentiary when the crime was committed."

Colons and Semicolons

Colons and semicolons go outside punctuation marks.

Marion said, "This hybrid automobile contains new technology"; David said, "The technology has been around for ten years."

Other Punctuation Marks

Question marks, exclamation points, dashes, parentheses and others go either inside or outside punctuation marks depending on their usage.

(Inside):   Sahir asked if I had read the article "Sonnet 18: Shall I Compare Thee to a Summer's day?"

(Outside):   Tim asked, "Have you seen my car keys"?

Italics (ital)

Today's word processing programs can create italics with the click of a mouse. Go to the toolbar and click on the *I* icon. That will italicize whatever you trying to draw attention to or emphasize. In the past, italics were not easy to produce by typewriters or handwriting. Consequently, italics were performed by underlining. Some still prefer doing so by going to the same toolbar and clicking on the U icon. Italics are used for the following:

Titles (of)

(Books):   *A Tale of Two Cities* or *A Tale of Two Cities; Bonfire of the Vanities* or *Bonfire of the Vanities*

(Plays):   *A Raisin in the Sun* or *A Raisin in the Sun; The Importance of Being Earnest* or *The Importance of Being Earnest*

(Magazines):   *Newsweek* or *Newsweek; Vogue* or *Vogue*
(Long poems):   *In Memoriam* or *In Memoriam; Beowulf* or *Beowulf*
(Pamphlets):   *The Use of the University Library* or *The Use of the University Library; Student Orientation Guide* or *Student Orientation Guide*
(Newspapers):   *The Washington Post* or *The Washington Post; The Tuscaloosa News* or *The Tuscaloosa News*

(Films):	*Big Momma's House* or *The Big Momma's House; Sixth Sense* or *Sixth Sense*
(Television programs):	*Law and Order* or *Law and Order; Seinfeld* or *Seinfeld*
(Paintings):	*The Whistler's Mother* or *The Whistler's Mother; The Kiss* or *The Kiss*
(Musical CD):	*The Best of Ravi Shankar* or *The Best Ravik 3* or *Punk Rock 3*
(Cartoons or comic strips):	*Cathy* or *Cathy; Garfield* or *Garfield*
(Software):	*PowerPoint* or *PowerPoint; MS Word* or *MS Word*
(Websites):	*Galileo* or *Galileo; Snopes* or *Snopes*

Note: Avoid italicizing or underlining the Bible or titles of legal documents, such as the Constitution of the People's Republic of Bangladesh.

Names (of)

Italicize or underline of the names of ships, aircrafts, trains, and spacecraft.

(Ships):	*Titanic* or *Titanic; HMS Nautilus* or *HMS Nautilus*
(Aircraft):	*The Spirit of St. Louis* or *The Spirit of St. Louis;*
(Trains):	*Amtrak Silver Star* or *Amtrak Silver Star; Broadway Limited* or *Broadway Limited*
(Spacecrafts):	*Apollo XIII* or *Apollo XIII; Challenger* or *Challenger*

Foreign Terms

Many foreign words and phrases are italicized. Do not italicize
or underline those terms that have become part of the English
language. If you are unsure, consult your dictionary.

(Italicized foreign terms)   :summa cum laude or (means with the
                                    highest honor); carpe diem or *carpe
                                    diem* (meaning seize the day); quid
                                    pro quo or *quid pro quo* (an equal
                                    exchange)

Capitalization (cap)

Writing a good essay requires the use of capital letters where they
are appropriate. Learning the use of capitalization is a good idea.

First Word of a Sentence

Use a capital letter to begin a new sentence.
Tornadoes cause death and destruction throughout the United
States.

Proper Nouns

The names of people, places, and products are capitalized. Many
have a tendency to capitalize common nouns, such as job titles and
college major and subjects, which is incorrect.

(Names of people):   Nadia, Tara, and Phil dove into the
                            swimming pool.
(Names of places):   My flight will stop at Amsterdam
                            and Frankfurt at JFK Airport.
(Name of products):   GM, Ford, and DaimlerChrysler are
                            losing sales of automobiles to the
                            Japanese manufacturers.
(Names of days of the
weeks, months, and holidays):   Friday, August, and Thanksgiving

| (Languages): | German, Bangla or Bengali, Mandarin Chinese |
| (Religions, organizations, nationalities, and races): | Buddhism, NATO, Bosnians, and Caucasians |

Titles

Use capital letters for the main words in titles of books, movies, television shows, songs, articles, chapters, poems, stories, papers, stage shows, and art works. Main words consist of nouns, adjectives, adverbs, and verbs. Minor words (articles, prepositions, and coordinating conjunctions) are not capitalized; unless, they come at the beginning or end of the title.

(Book):	*The Encyclopedia of Gods*
(Book with a subtitle):	*The Bedford Anthology of World Literature: The Middle Period, 100 C.E.-1400*
(Poem):	"Sailing to Byzantium"
(Articles):	"Obesity is an American Phenomenon"

Titles of Persons

Capital letters are used for titles of people when they come at the beginning of a name, not after.

| (At the beginning): | Mayor Lois Brown won her re-election by a landslide., Dr. Canor easts lunch in his office. Professor Kaul teaches journalism. |
| (After): | Lois Brown, the mayor of Sommerville, won her re-election by a landslide. The doctor eats lunch in his office. The professor teaches journalism. |

Abbreviations (abr)

Abbreviations are shortened versions of some words. Use them in moderation. Taking shortcuts in formal writing is irritating to the readers. Some of them are as follows: California (not Cali); ounce (for oz); February (not Feb.); page (not p.); and others.

Titles

Abbreviations are used after or before people's names.

(Before):   Rev. Joseph Manley, Dr. Sumita Patel. Ms. Amy Cooper, Mr. Solomon Shepherd

(After):   Richard Johnson, C.P.A.; James Harmon, D.D.S; Iqbal Ahmed, Ph.D.; Wendy Thomas, D.V.M.; Raymond James, Jr.

Initials

Abbreviations are used for initials in names.

R.C. Thomas, Steve A, Gray, J. Allen Wilson

Time, number, and amount indicators

Abbreviations are with dates and times, numbers, and amounts.

(Dates):   700 BC (before Christ) of 700 BCE (before the common era) AD 1578 (anno Domini or the year of our Lord) or 1578 CE (common era)
(Time):   5:00 A.M. or a.m. (ante meridiem)
                 7:00 P.M. or p.m. (post meridiem)
(Number):   She lived in apartment No. 9.
(Amount):   Gerald borrowed $100 from his brother.

Well-known Organizations and Businesses

Abbreviations are used to denote organizations that are well known in their abbreviated forms. Write the entire name of the organization that is not commonly recognized, followed by the abbreviation of it all capital letters inside parentheses. Afterwards, the abbreviation can be used.

| (Well-known organizations): | IRS, FBI, CIA, at&t, NAACP, YMCA, ATM, IBM |

(Not well-known organizations): Agents of the Tennessee Bureau of Investigation (TBI) inspected the crime scene.

Latin abbreviations

Latin abbreviations are good for informal writing and bibliographic entries. In general, writers avoid them.

Abbreviation	Latin expression	English denotation
Cf.	confer	compare
e.g.	exempli gratia	for example
et al	et alia	and others
etc.	et cetera	and so forth
i.e.	id est	that is
N.B.	nota bene	note well

Numbers (num)

The use of numbers in essays requires special care. Below are some of the generally accepted guidelines

Numbers Written in One or Two Words

Numbers written in one or two words are usually spelled out. Larger numbers are written out in Arabic numerals.

(One or two words): The child had eight toys.

(More than two words):   More than 200 diamond rings were
                           stolen from the jewelry store.

Numbers Beginning Sentences

Sentences beginning with numbers are written out..

(Number):   Two hundred and fifty-five students joined
                           the protest against the increase of tuition
                           at their college.

Consistency

Within a sentence, if there are one or more numbers that will be
numerals, all of the numbers should follow a consistent pattern that
is written as numerals.

He needed 60 hours to graduate, while Bobby needed 112 hours.

Numerical References

Numerals are used for the following numerical references:

(Dates):   March 21, 1910, 700 AD

(Time):   7:30 a.m. or seven o'clock (When the term
                           o'clcok is used, the number is written
                           out.)

(Decimals, fractions, and
percentages):   5.5; ¼; 15 percent (15 %)
(Chapter and page numbers): chapter 5; page 40; pages 10-12;
                           pages A1, A16

(Street number and zip code):   47 Wood Duck Cove, Jackson,
                           TN 38305

(Telephone number):   901-555-0101

(Money): $20.50; 0.75 cents;

Spelling (sp)

Spelling in the English language is one of the most convoluted ones because of the language's liberal policy of welcoming words and phrases from other languages. In the United States, immigration from different parts of the world has added to the confusion. French, Italian, African, Irish, Dutch, Spanish, and other languages have changed English to create the distinct American English. Moreover, the language has over the centuries borrowed heavily from German, Greek, Latin, and otherIndo-European languages. Thus, it is difficult to teach English spelling, as there are exceptions to almost every spelling rule. One way to know how to spell reasonably well is to learn some of the basic rules, and rely on a good dictionary—not the spell checker on the computer. Spell check is not that thorough and unnecessarily puts a red squiggly line under spellings which is not in its storage. Bad spelling is not looked upon kindly. In fact, it diminishes a writer's credibility. The tips below should help you. Above all, you have to take the initiative to become skilled in spelling.

The *i* before the *e* Rule

The rule is *i before e*, except for *c*, or when the word sounds like *a* in *weigh* and *neighbor.*

(I before E):	believe, relieve, achieve, friend, field
(E before I after C):	receive, deceive, ceiling, conceive
(a sound):	eight, neighbor, weigh, vein

The silent *e* Rule

The rule drops the silent *e* in words when the suffix starts with vowels. The *e* stays when the suffixes start with consonants

(Suffixes with vowels):	confuse + ing = confusing; hope + ing = hoping
(Suffixes with consonants):	hope + ful = hopeful; true + ly = truly

The *y* Rule

The rule is to change the *y* to *i* and *es* for words ending in *y* followed by consonants but not so for words followed by vowels.

(Consonants):   dry + ed = dried; theory + es = theories; tragedy +es = tragedies

(Vowels):   display + ed = displayed; carry + ing = carrying; destroy + s = destroys

The Double Consonant RuleThe rule is to double the consonants: for words ending in a single consonant after a single vowel, followed by a single consonant; the word is only one syllable or the accent is on the last syllable; and the suffix starts with a vowel.

(Single Consonant, Single Vowel, Single Consonant): begin + ing

(One syllable or accent
 is on last syllable):   stop + ed = stopped
(Suffix starts with a vowel): occur + ence: occurrence

Plurals

Several rules apply to form plurals. They are listed below.

Addition of *s*

Most plurals are formed by adding *s* to singular nouns.

phone to phones; clock to clocks; table to tables

Addition of *es*

Singular nouns that end in *s, sh, ch, x,* or *z* form plurals by adding *es*. In addition, *es* is added to words that end in *f* or *fe* by dropping them and substituting *v* for the *f* or *fe*.

(*s, , sh, ch, x,* or *z* endings):   class to classes; dish to dishes; watch to watches, box to boxes, buzz to buzz

(*f* or *fe* endings):   thief to thieves; wife to wives

Change of Spelling

The English language has a number of words that change their spellings in the plural form. Nouns derived from Greek, Latin, and French languages change to the plural forms in their original forms.

(Irregular plurals):   man to men; goose to geese (not moose to meese); mouse to mice

(Derivative nouns):   curriculum to curricula; medium to media; fabliaux to fabliau

No Change of Spelling

Some words remain the same in both the singular and plural forms. A few such words are as follows:

Singular	Plural
deer	deer
fish	fish
moose	moose
sheep	sheep
species	species

Homonyms

A group of words that give a numbers of students spelling headaches is called homonyms or homophones. Homonyms are

words that sound alike but have different meanings and spellings.
The following are some homonyms that give the most trouble.

accept	(verb) to receive; to accept
except	(preposition) to leave out; but
advice	(noun) suggestion
advise	(verb) counsel; to recommend
affect	(verb) influence; impress
effect	(noun) outcome; result
allude	(verb) make disguised reference
elude	(verb) evade; escape
already	(adverb) before specified time
all ready	(adverb) fixed; arranged
allusion	(noun) indirect reference
illusion	(noun) misleading image
a lot	(adverb) several; much
allot	(verb) assign
brake	(verb) to stop: (noun) a stopping apparatus
break	(verb) crack; smash
choose	(verb) pick out; select
chose	(verb) to have picket out or selected
cite	(verb) to quote; assert
sight	(noun) view; (verb) see
site	(noun) place; location
clothes	(noun) apparel; garments
cloths	(noun) fabric
coarse	(adjective) rough; rude
course	(noun) academic study; path
conscience	(noun) morals
conscious	(adjective) alert; intentional
dairy	(noun) milk producer
diary	(noun) daily record

desert	(noun) barren and sandy place; (verb) abandon
dessert	(noun) final course of meal
does	(verb) carrying out
dose	(noun) portion
elicit	(verb) bring out
illicit	(adjective) illegal
eminent	(adjective) prestigious
imminent	(adjective) near; forthcoming
envelop	(verb) to cover
envelope	(noun) paper pouch
fair	(adjective) impartial; mediocre; beautiful; (noun) carnival
fare	(noun) price for passage; meal; (verb) get along
gorilla	(noun) monkey
guerrilla	(noun) unconventional soldier
human	(noun) person; (adjective) civilized
humane	(adjective) forgiving; charitable
its	(pronoun) belonging
it's	(contraction) of it is
lead	(noun) a heavy metal; (verb) guide
led	(verb) past tense of lead
loose	(adjective) not tight; liberated
lose	(verb) mislay; defeated
passed	(verb) allowed; gone ahead
past	(adjective) former; (noun) time gone by
pair	(noun) two
pare	(verb) peel
patience	(noun) endurance; perseverance
patient	(noun) sick person; (adjective) enduring
personal	(adjective) private
personnel	(noun) employees

principal	(noun) main; head of a school
principle	(noun) guideline; rule
quiet	(adjective) noiseless
quite	(adverb) completely; to an extent
rain	(noun) cloudburst
reign	(noun) rule
rein	(verb) control
right	(adjective) appropriate; opposite of left
rite	(noun) ceremony
write	(verb) to put words down on any surface
sense	(noun) feeling; awareness
since	(adverb) ago; (preposition) because
than	(preposition) exceeding
then	((adverb) before
their	(pronoun) belonging to them
there	(adverb) position
they're	(contraction) they are
to	(preposition) toward; (infinitive verb) as *to* study
too	(adverb) also
two	(noun) the number 2
threw	(verb) hurled (past tense of throw)
through	(adjective) finished; one way
thorough	(adjective) exhaustive
weather	(noun) meteorological outlook; (verb) endure
whether	(conjunction) in the case that
whose	(pronoun) possessive form of *who*
who's	(contraction) of *who is*
were	(verb) past tense of *are*
where	(noun) location
your	(adjective) possessive form of *you*
you're	(pronoun) contraction of *you are*

Vowels

Vowels give people problems. Vowels are *a, e, i, o, u,* or the silent *h* sound. The rule is to use the article *an* in front of a singular word with a vowel sound. On the other hand, the article *a* is used for a singular word with a consonant.

(Vowels):   an apple, an aunt, an hour

(Consonants):   a table, a calculator, a vision

Clichés

Clichés are overused metaphors or sayings. As a fresh one, a metaphor is useful in writing but loses its freshness from excessive use. In a conversation, most people do not mind the clichés. By contrast, they get irritated with them while reading them—making them think that you lack creativity. Avoid getting labeled a dull and boring writer. Below is a collection of clichés. By all means avoid them.

a barrel of monkeys

a fish out of water

a force to be reckoned with

as hard to find as needle in a haystack

avoid like the plague

beat around the bush

blow your own horn

born with a sliver spoon in his mouth

busy as a bee

claw to the top

cool as a cucumber

cold as ice

couldn't care less

crazy like a fox

crystal clear

dead as a doornail

does my heart good

dog tired

don't count your chickens before they are hatched

drive like a maniac

drove a stake through the heart

dumb blonde

easier said than done

flat as a pancake

fog as thick as pea soup

good as gold

green as grass

happy as a clam

handwriting on the wall

hard as nails

head over heels in love

in the nick of time

in times of trouble

it goes without saying

it's better to have loved and lost than never to loved at all

keep your fingers crossed

last but not least

light as a feather

like a bull in a china shop

like a chicken with its head cut off

live off the fat of the land

meek as a lamb

more power to you

movers and shakers

old as the hills

out of the frying pan into the fire

playing with fire

pretty as a picture

quick as lightning

pull out all the stops

quick as a flash

rain or shine

raining cats and dogs

read the riot act

rise and shine

rooted to the spot

ripped to shreds

rocket science

short and sweet

sigh of relief

silent as the grave

smart as a whip

solid as the rock of Gibraltar

starting out at the bottom of the ladder

tame a wild beast

tried and true

up the river without a paddle

unvarnished truth

water under the bridge

whisper sweet nothings

white as a ghost

without a doubt

Jargons

Every profession, sports, and special group has its own language.
The Internet and people in technology are also responsible for
infecting the English language with numerous jargons. For

physicians and lawyers, the use of jargons gives them a sense of prestige. A physician may say to his or her patient, "You need immediate surgery for your *deviated septum*." The patient has little understanding of the term and panics about his or her physical condition. *Deviated septum* means abnormal displacement of the nasal cavity—not a very serious problem. If the physician had used common English terms, the patient would be far less worried. Similarly, a lawyer could say, "That case would require *pro bono* work, and I do not do that." *Pro bono* means legal work that is done without compensation. Some jargons, used online, are as follows:

2L8	(too late)
B4N	(bye for now)
CUL	(see you later)
flame	(an angry or rude email)
IMAP	(Internet message access protocol)
IMHO	(in my humble opinion)
LOL	(laugh out loud)
Mailer daemon	(bounced email—when email comes back to the sender)
netiquette	(network etiquette)
ROTL	(roll on the floor laughing)
SIG	(special interest group)
SPAM	(unsolicited commercial email)
TIA	(thanks in advance)

Other jargons also abound in our language. They are commonly used in the United States. (A few of them and their normal terms are provided below.) Avoid using them and others in your writing.

commence	(to begin)
facilitate	(help bring about)
impact	(effect or impression)
optimum	(most favorable or advantageous)
peruse	(to read or examine)
prioritize	(to arrange or deal with in order of importance)
utilize	(use)
viable	(successful or effective)

Slangs

Slangs are a popular means of communication for many people, but in writing they are to be avoided. This form of language is short lived and used as substitute for standard terms in order to be playful, humorous, and important. Problems with the use of slangs are two fold. First, they change rapidly. A term that had been popular at one time might lose its currency after a while. For instance, the term *groovy*—popular a few decades ago—is hardly heard these days. Second, slangs take on a regional tone. Popular in one area, certain made up words and phrases might be completely misunderstood in other parts of the country or other speakers of the language. Examples of regionalism can be shown by two terms used in the South. The first is the word *fixing*. In the South, everybody is *fixing* to do something. My mother is *fixing* to go shopping, or Maria is *fixing* dinner. An extreme example is the term *mama an 'em*, used thus: How is your *mama an 'em?*

The question is inquiring about the welfare of the listener's mother and the rest of the family. Below are a few of the countless slangs that you are likely to come across.

Slang	*Meaning*
airhead	stupid person
awesome	great
bad	intense, good
beemer	BMW automobile
big mouth	talks too much
cold fish	dull
cool	good
couch potato	lazy person
dicey	chancy
dork	strange person
eating away	bothering
far out	great
fox	attractive
glitch	problem
grass	marijuana
hang loose	relax
ho	prostitute
intense	serious
just of the boat	naïve
kooks	strange people

loser	annoying person
maxed out	exhausted
negatives	bad things
nuts	crazy
party animal	lover of parties
plastered	intoxicated
rap	talk about
rug rats	children
screw up	make a mistake
stressed	upset
totaled	completely wrecked
up for grabs	available
vibes	feelings
wheels	car
zip	nothing

Similes and metaphors

You have been asked to avoid colloquialisms, slangs, clichés, or jargons, but you can make your writing lively through the use of figurative language. This style is a creative, not a literal, way of expressing abstract terms through the use of similes and metaphors.

Similes

Similes are comparisons of two dissimilar things by using *like* or *as.*

His ears were like two conch shells. (Here the *ears* are being compared to *conch shells*—two unlike things.)

Metaphors

Metaphors are comparisons of two dissimilar things without using *like* or *as.*

His ears are conch shells. (Here the *ears* are compared to *conch shells* without using *like* as in the case of the example for similes.)

Modifiers

Modifiers are words, phrases, or clauses that describe other words and require proper use. If not, modifiers can cause difficulties for beginning writers. Two common errors are misplaced modifiers and dangling modifiers.

Misplaced modifiers

When words or phrases are not close to the words they describe, they cause the misplacement of modifiers—sometimes resulting in humorous meanings. By moving the words and phrases near the words they are describing, misplaced modifiers can be corrected.

(Misplaced words):   The guests almost ate all of Martha's pecan pie.

(Correct):   The guests ate almost all of Martha's pecan pie.

(Misplaced phrases):   I ran into the deer with a car.

(Correct):   I ran into a deer with the car I was driving.

Dangling modifiers (dm)

Dangling modifiers also cause humorous language. They usually occur at the beginning of sentences, modifying words not clearly stated. Two methods can be used to correct dangling modifiers.

1. Place the subject immediately following the introductory word group.

2. Place a subject and verb in the opening word group.

(Incorrect):

(Misplaced clause):   While eating breakfast, the rain came down.

(Correct):   While I was eating breakfast, the rain came down.

(Correct):   The rain came down while I was eating breakfast.

Adjectives (adj)

Adjectives are words that describe or modify nouns or pronouns. Some adjectives come in front of their nouns and others behind them, while some are even separated from the nouns they are describing. Words such as these are adjectives.

(Adjectives):   red, magnificent, rainy, scrawny, striped

(Before nouns):   *red* apple, *magnificent* performance, *scrawny* lion, *striped* tiger

(After the noun):   his hunger *satiated*

(Separated from the noun): The victory was *robust.*

Comparative Adjectives

When adjectives are used to perform comparisons, they change their spellings. For comparing two items, adjectives (usually of one syllable) add the suffix *er* to it. A three item comparison adds the suffix *est.* As rules have exceptions, some adjectives take on different forms without adding *er* or *est* to them. Furthermore, some adjectives do not change spellings when they are being compared. In comparing two items, the adjectives will take the word *more;* three-item comparisons will take the word *most.*

Adjectives	*er form*	*est form*
wet	wetter	wettest
great	greater	greatest
bright	brighter	brightest
few	fewer	fewest

(More and most): The Audi has *more* horsepower than the Buick, but the Aston Martin has the *most* horsepower.

Adjectives	*Comparison of two*	*Comparison of three*
bad	worse	worst
good, well	better	best
little	less	least
much, many	more	most

Adverbs (adv)

Adverbs modify verbs, adjectives, other adverbs, phrases, or clauses. Generally, adverbs usually end in the *ly* suffix and answer questions such as how, when, where, and how much.

(Adverbs with *ly* suffix):   quickly, efficiently, badly, patiently

(Modifier of the verb *jumped*):   I *quickly* jumped over the fence as the dog chased me.

(Modifier of the adjective *happy*): Moin is *truly* happy for getting
the promotion.

(Modifier of the adverb *cautiously*): Electricians work *very*
cautiously.

(*Consequently* as modifier of the
sentence):   *Consequently*, all charges were
dropped against the teenager.

Too many times the adjective *good* is used instead of the adverb
well. Other adjectives are also used in place of adverbs.

(Incorrect use of *good*): I feel *good.*

(Correct use of *well*):   I feel *well.* (The adverb is properly
modifying the verb *feel.*)

(Incorrect):   She drives *slow* in the fast lane. (*Slow* is an
adjective and cannot perform the function
of an adverb.)

(Correct):   She drives *slowly* in the fast lane.

Prepositions (prep)

Prepositions are used before nouns to provide additional
information in sentences. Most of the time, prepositions are used
for showing directions or relationships. Some of the most common
prepositions are listed below.

about	beneath	into	through
above	beside	like	to
across	between	near	toward
after	by	of	under
along	despite	off	underneath
among	down	on	unlike
around	during	onto	until
at	except	out	up
before	for	outside	upon
behind	from	over	with
below	in	past	without

Prepositional phrases

Prepositional phrases are made of prepositions and their objects—noun and pronouns that follow them—as well as any modifiers to related to either one of them.

She will come here *before 5 o'clock.*

The student government association president was *in favor of a new parking deck for the campus.* (In this example, there are three prepositional phrases.)
Because of sleet, schools were closed.

Conjunctions (conj)

Conjunctions join words, phrases, clauses, or sentences.

Coordinating conjunctions

Coordinating conjunctions, preceded by commas, are used for joining two independent conjunctions to form compound sentences. In fact, coordinating conjunctions join two equal parts. The coordinating conjunctions are *and, but, for, nor, or, so, yet.* An easy way to remember them is through the acronym FANBOYS.

F—for

A—an

N—nor

B—but

Avoid starting sentences with coordinating conjunctions. Remember, coordinating conjunctions are connectors. As such, they have nothing to link with as the first word of a sentence.

Correlative conjunctions

Correlative conjunctions appear in pairs to join equal parts. These are correlative conjunctions:

either/or
neither/nor
not only/but also
whether/or

Subordinating conjunctions

Subordinating conjunctions join dependent clauses to independent clauses to form complex sentences. (See complex sentences in the chapter on Writing.) The following is a list of some coordinating conjunctions.

after, although, how, till (or 'til), although, if, unless, as, inasmuch, until, as if, in order, that, when, as long as, lest, when, whenever, as much as, now that, where, as soon as, provided (that), wherever, as though, since, while, because, so that, before, than, even if, that, even though, though, where, whether, while, rather than

Expletives

Expletives have no meanings and are used at the beginning of sentences to simply meaning to the sentences. Two expletives are *there* and *it*. *There* (*is, was, were*) indicates a position or feelings of satisfaction, relief, sympathy, or anger. *It* (*is, was*), on the other hand, is used for emphasis on the subject of a verb. The use of too many expletives is not recommended in your writing because they contribute wordiness. (See section on <u>wordiness</u>.)

(There: Position):	*There* is a dog on the front lawn.
(There: Feelings):	*There*, be happy with your gift.
(It: Emphasis):	*It* is a beautiful day.

Interjections (int)

Interjections exhibit emotion, excitement or surprise. They are hardly used in scholarly and business writing. Moreover, commas and exclamation points are used after interjections.

Ah, that is what I wanted.
Ouch, you touched my sore.
Oh, I failed to see the dog.
Hey! Wait for me!
Well, that is the price you pay for being careless.

Points of View

Points of view are the positions from which things are observed or regarded. There are three of them: first person (*I* or *we*), second person (*you*), and third person *(he, she, it, they)*. Students have a tendency to use the first person *I* and second person *you* in almost every composition they write. The first person is generally a great perspective for autobiographical writing (personal experience). The second person is useful for process essays. (See the chapter on writing for an explanation of process essays.) The third person is the point of view of objective or unbiased writers, who avoid personal narratives. Therefore, the third person might be more appropriate because of its use in scholarly writing, such as, discussing the development of the software industry in India. Beginning writers shift points of view, without realizing it. Care must be taken to stay with one of them, depending on the topic. If you have questions about the appropriateness of the point of view, seek advice from your instructor.

Choppy Sentences

A bunch of simple sentences (see simple sentences in the chapter on writing), one after the other, tend to make most writing choppy. Such narratives will sound like four radial tires on a car driving over a concrete bridge—making annoying noise. The prescription for fixing choppiness is by combing sentences, either by forming compound sentences or subordinating some to others.

Voice

Sentences can take the active or the passive form. In the active voice, the subject performs the action. However, in the passive voice the subject is acted upon. The subject in this case can be less important than the action it is performing or the subject is itself unidentified. It is preferable to use the active voice in writing because of its clarity and straightforwardness. Moreover, writing in active voice uses fewer words. Passive sentences have their place in writing because they provide variety and sometimes emphases, too.

(Passive voice):　　　The homework was eaten by the dog.
(Active voice):　　　The dog ate the homework. (In this example, the sentence uses two fewer words than the example of the passive sentence.)

Parallelism

Parallelism problems result from unequal treatment of comparable ideas in a sentence. In order for sentences to flow smoothly, they should contain parallel structures. This type of structure treats words, phrases, or clauses in a similar manner. Typically, parallel structures are joined together with coordinating conjunctions. (See coordinating conjunctions in this section.)

Words and phrases
Words and phrases must be in parallel forms.

(Incorrect *ing* gerund form):　　Alan likes swimming, flying, and to read.
(Correct *ing* gerund form):　　Alan likes swimming, flying, and reading.
(Incorrect infinitive form):　　The puppy likes to play, to eat, and sleeping.
(Correct infinitive form):　　The puppy likes to play, to eat, and to sleep. (*To* can be used for each of the parallel words, or it can be used once in front of the first parallel word: The puppy likes to play, eat, and sleep.)

Clauses

All clauses in sentences must be in parallel forms. Changing verb tense (See verb tense in this Section.) or voice (See voice in this Sectiom.) from active to passive or the other way round will stop from achieving parallelism.

(Incorrect):   The mother told her teenagers that
                          they should come home early, that
                          they should eat healthy meals, and
                          be involved in community service.

(Correct):   The mother told her teenagers that
                          they should come   home early, that
                          they should eat healthy meals, and
                          that they should be involved in
                          community service.

Lists

Lists that follow colons (See this chapter for colons.) should be in parallel form.

(Incorrect):   We studied the following of types of
                          plays last semester: tragedies,
                          comedies, and dramas known as
                          tragic- comedies.

(Correct):   We studied the following of types of
                          plays last semester: tragedies,
                          comedies, and tragic-comedies.

Nominalizations

Nominalizations are nouns derived from verbs and adjectives. Ordinarily, these nouns take the following suffixes: *ance, ence, ion, ing,* or *ment.* Since nominalizations are a part of our language, they are not always troublesome. However, they rob the characteristics of good composition—clarity and brevity. The best way to fix nominalizations is to turn them into action verbs.

appear (verb) to appear*ance*
differ (adjective) to differ*ence*
compete (verb) to competit*ion*
meet (verb) to meet*ing*
establish (verb) establish*ment*

(Weak use of *appearance*):	I made my *appearance* at the meeting as it was beginning.
(Better use of *appeared*):	I *appeared* at the meeting as it was beginning.
(Weak use of *difference*):	The *difference* between the two is how they dress.
(Better use of *differ*):	They differ in the way they dress.
(Weak use of *competition*):	The US soccer team faced stiff *competition* in the World Cup.
(Better use if *competed*):	The US soccer team *competed* against strong teams in the World Cup.
(Weak use of *meeting*):	Walter is *meeting* me at the library.
(Better use of *meet*):	Walter will *meet* me at the library.
(Weak use of *establishment*):	The establishment of rules will help the organization in its mission.
(Better use of *establish*):	*Establish* rules, and they will help the organization's mission.

Repetition (rep)

Generally, repetition makes writing dull. In public speaking, by contrast, repetition is prized because audience members have poor listening habits. Guidelines in public speaking say: Tell them what you are going to tell them; tell them; tell them what you told them. Repetition can be eliminated by following these guidelines:

1. Use of the same word over and over again;
2. use of sentences of the same type;
3. use of sentences of the same length;
4. use of the same type of sentence openings;
5. use of passive voice;
6. use of the same subject; and
7. use of *there is* and *it is.*

In spite of the caution in the judicious use of repetition, it has a role in essays. Repetition emphasizes feelings, thoughts, and ideas.

Variety *(var)*

Variety produces freshness in writing. In a number of ways essays can become interesting:

1. By varying openings of sentences;
2. by varying types of sentences;
3. by varying length of sentences;
4. by varying length of paragraphs; and
5. by varying the opening sentence of each paragraph.

Do not tell

Sometimes students write in their introductory paragraph what they intend to do in the rest of their essay. Frequently, they make a statement similar to this one: "I will show you how *Beowulf* is considered to be a work of Christian symbolism." This kind of proclamation rarely sits well with the readers. Readers feel, "Hey, I am not a dummy. I can figure out the contents of your essay from your thesis statement and body paragraphs." Thus, remember to show—not to tell.

Usage (usage)

Some words and phrases often cause problems for writers. The glossary below provides in an alphabetical order some of those terms. In addition, expressions commonly labeled as colloquialisms, slangs, and jargons are also in this list, although some of them have been discussed elsewhere in this or other sections of the book. If you have you have doubts about proper usage, always consult a dictionary.

a, an:	(See vowels in this Section.)
accept, except:	(See homonyms in this Section.)
adapt, adopt:	*Adapt* is a verb meaning "to make suitable for use for a purpose." *Adopt* is a verb meaning "to take

and make one's own," as in this example: I will easily *adapt* to the Japanese lifestyle because I am aware of many of their customs. We want to *adopt* to a child.

advice, advise: (See homonyms in this Section.)

affect, effect: (See homonyms in this Section.)

a lot, allot: (See homonyms in this Section.)

already, all ready: (See homonyms in this Section.)

all right, alright: *All right* is standard form—not *alright.* As an i adjective, *all right* means "acceptable or greeable," as in this example: David is *all right* now after collapsing on the football field. As an adverb, *all right* means satisfactory, as in this example: Lupe is all right with the agreement.

all together, altogether: *All together* is an adverb meaning "to gather together," as in this example: We will arrive at the barbeque *all together.* *Altogether* is an adverb meaning "completely," as in this example: The pages of the research paper were altogether.

allude, elude: (See homonyms in this Section.)

allusion, illusion: (See homonyms in this Section.)

almost, most: *Almost* is an adverb meaning "nearly," as in this example: Chad was *almost* home when he the pickup truck hit his car. *Most* is an adjective meaning "many," as in this example: *Most* of the students were absent from Dr. Thomas' class.

among, between: *Among* is a preposition that shows relationships of three or more people or things, as in this example: The millionaire distributed his money *among* all four of his children. *Between* is a preposition meaning the "interval or equidistance of two people or things," as in this example: The dispute *between* Tom and Beth was settled today, amount, number: *Amount* is a noun meaning quantity that cannot be counted as separate units, such as water, milk, or sand, as in this example: A large *amount* of sand was dumped on the driveway. *Number,* on the other hand, is used for counting individual items, such as people, as in this example: A number of people said that they witnessed the accident.

anxious, eager: *Anxious* is an adjective meaning "worried," as in this example: Professor Miller's class was *anxious* about the final examination. *Eager* is a noun meaning "keen interest," as in this example: The detectives were *eager* to examine the crime scene.

anybody, anyone: (See pronouns in this Section.)

anymore, any more: *Anymore* is an adverb meaning "now," as in this example: Does she know anymore where she lost her purse? *Any more* is a noun meaning "a greater amount," as in this example: He refused *any more* food. Note that both anymore and any more are used in a negative manner.

anxious, eager: *Anxious* is an adjective meaning "worried," as in this example: The residents of Tampa were anxious about the hurricane in the Gulf of Mexico. *Eager* is an adjective meaning "showing keen interest," as in this example: The students were

eager to dissect the frog. as, like:
As is a conjunction meaning "in equal degree," as in this example: Autumn was hot *as* summer. *Like* is a preposition meaning "resembling," as in this example: Josephine sings like she is Lena Horne. Such use of *like* is unacceptable in standard English, so the sentence can be rewritten in this manner: Josephine sings as if she is Lena Horne.

awful, awfully: *Awful* is an adjective meaning "terrible," as in this example: The *awful* clothes made look a someone from the sixties. *Awfully* is an adverb meaning "very or extreme," as in this example: She is *awfully* hungry.

a while, awhile: *A while* is an article and a noun meaning "a longer period," as in this example: Dr. Baxter will be gone for *a while*. *Awhile* is an adverb meaning " for a shorter period," as in this example: They decided to stay *awhile*. (*Awhile* cannot be preceded by a preposition such as *for*; *a while* has no such restriction.)

bad, badly: *Bad* is an adjective meaning "unfavorable," as in this example: The *bad* boy knocked down the mail boxes in the neighborhood. *Badly* is an adverb meaning "in a worse way," as in this example: My college team was *badly* beaten. being that, being as: Both of these terms are colloquial expressions and are to be avoided. The substitutes for them are *because* or *since*.

(Incorrect):   *Being that* Ted sleeps late, he misses the morning television shows.

(Correct):	*Because* Ted sleeps late, he missed the morning television shows.
beside, besides:	*Beside* is a preposition meaning "next to," as in this example: Dexter parked his car beside the Rolls Royce. *Besides* is also a preposition meaning "in addition to" or "except for," as in this example: Besides Miranda, Michael will join the organization.
bring, take:	*Bring* is a verb meaning "to move something forward," as in this example: Melanie promised to *bring* her book to class. *Take* is a verb meaning to "move something away," as in this example: Mario promised to *take* his furniture when he moves to New York.
burst, bursted:	*Burst* is a verb meaning "come open or explode violently." *Bursted* is a non-standard form and should be avoided.
(Incorrect):	A truck *bursted* into flames.
(Correct):	A truck burst into flames.can,
may:	*Can* is a verb (in this case) meaning
"ability" or "capability," as in this example:	The group *can* easily meet the deadline. *May* is a verb (in this case) meaning "to allow," as in this example: *May* I see you in my office? (*Can* is used for showing ability and *may* for seeking permission.)
censor, censure:	*Censor* is a verb (in this case) meaning "to examine and delete," as in this example: The editor will *censor* the television because of its adult content. Censure is a verb meaning "official rebuke," as in this example: The congressman was *censured* for unethical fund raising.

cite, sight, site:	*Cite* is a verb meaning to "commend," or "quote. (Commend): The firefighter was *cited* for rescuing the woman from the burning house. (Quote): The professor asked her to *cite* the passage in the essay. *Sight* is a noun meaning "ability to see," or "view." (Ability to see): People lose their eye *sight* when they get older. (View): The soldier fired his gun when the enemy appeared in his *sight. Site* is a noun meaning "a place" or "location," as in this example: The building *site* is full of construction workers.
climactic, climatic:	*Climactic* is an adjective meaning "related to climate," a as in this example: Climactic changes have precipitated a heat wave this summer all over the world . *Climatic* is an adjective meaning "causing a climax," as in this example: The discovery of the cave was a *climactic* end to our trek though the forest.
coarse, course:	(See homonyms in this Section.)
complement, compliment	: *Complement* is a noun meaning "to add," as in this example Bottled water *complements* the company's line of soft drinks. *Compliment* is a noun meaning "to praise," as in this example: Mr. Hightower receives compliments for his clothes.
conscious, conscience:	(See homonyms in this Section.)
continual, continuous:	*Continual* is an adjective meaning "occurring regularly," as in this example: The continual need to drive to work is bothering Andre. *Continuous* is an adjective meaning uninterrupted in time, sequence, or event," as in this example: The

continuous   barrage of mortar fire
kept him awake him last night.

could of:
Could of is a nonstandard term.
The proper term is *could have.*
Incorrect use of *could of*): They
could of finished cleaning the
bathrooms before the guests
arrived. (Correct use of *could
have*): They *could have* finished
cleaning the bathrooms before the
guests arrived.

criteria:
Criteria is a noun meaning "rules"
or "standards" and is the singular
form of *criterion.*

(*criteria*):
The *criteria* for judging the essay
contest are posted on the bulletin
board.

(criterion):
One *criterion* applies for the
promotion to become a supervisor.

data:
Data is a noun meaning "factual
information" or "numerical or other
information for processing by
computers" and is the plural form of
datum. Now *data* is acceptable for
both singular and plural forms,
although some still use *datum* as a
singular term.
    The stolen computer
contained sensitive *data.*

different from, different than:
Different from is the preferred term,
such as: All the brothers are
different from each other. However,
different than is also used to reduce
wordiness, as in this example: The
brothers are *different than* each
other.

disinterested, uninterested:
Disinterested is an adjective
meaning "impartial" or "unbiased,"
as in this example: We have to find
three *disinterested* people to judge
the beauty contest. *Uninterested* is

an adjective meaning "lack of interest," as in this example: Miguel was *uninterested* in buying a new car.

due to the fact that:
Due to the fact that is wordy term. It should be avoided and the preferred substitution is *because*. (Incorrect use of *due to the fact that*): *Due to the fact that* Cassandra is an engineer, she repairs her own cars. (Correct use of *because*): *Because* Cassandra is an engineer, she repairs her own cars.

elict, illict:
Elict is a verb meaning "to bring out," as in this example: Detective Harmon can elicit information from uncooperative suspects. *Illict* is an adjective meaning "unlawful," as in this example: After the hiring of several new police officers illict activities decreased.

emigrate, immigrate:
Emigrate is a verb meaning "leave one place to move to another," as in this example: People throughout history have emigrated from one area to another. *Immigrate* is a verb meaning "to move from one's country and settle in another," as in this example: People immigrate to the United States from all over the world.

eminent, imminent:
(See homonyms in this Section.)

enthused:
Enthused has not gained acceptance and is treated as a non-standard term, The proper expression is *enthusiastic*.

(Incorrect use of *enthused*):
Pat's father was *enthused* with his children's academic achievements.

(Correct use of *enthusiastic*):
Pat's father was *enthusiastic* about his children's academic

achievements.

every one, everyone: *Every one* is a pronoun meaning "each one" and must be followed by *of,* as in this example: We threw back into the river every one of the fish we caught. *Everyone* is a pronoun meaning "everybody," as in this example: *Everyone* is required to drive over the rough terrain to complete the race.

every body, everybody: *Every body* is a pronoun meaning "every one" and must be followed by *of* as in this example: *Every body* of the group was asked to produce identity cards. *Everybody* in the nursing home takes his or her medicine regularly.

farther, further: *Farther* is an adjective meaning "at a great distance," as in this example: She lives *farther* down the road. *Further* is an adjective meaning "more time, amount, or degree," as in this example: *Further,* the car needs its tires rotated.

fewer, less: *Fewer* is a noun meaning "small number of persons or things" and counted as separate units, as in this example: The orchard is producing *fewer* apples every year. *Less* is a noun meaning "smaller amount" and is used to count amounts that are not in separate units, as in this example: The waitress gave her less milk than I got.

firstly: *Firstly* is an adverb meaning "in the first place" and is advised not to be used. The proper term is *first.*

(Incorrect use of *firstly*):   *Firstly,* the employment manual mandates a fine for being late three times in a week.

(Correct use of *first*):   *First,* the employment manual

mandates a fine for being late three times in a week.

get:

Get is a verb meaning "to receive," as in this example: She *gets* flowers from her boyfriend every Friday. Used to mean "emotional response or reaction," *get* is considered to be a colloquialism and should be avoided, as in this example: News of cancer deaths *gets* me.

good, well:

(ee adverbs in this Section.)

graduate:

Graduate is a verb meaning "to have received a degree or diploma from an academic institution," as in this example: She is the first African American woman to *graduate* from Georgia Tech. It is incorrect to drop *from* after the use of *graduate* in a sentence, as in this example: She is the first African American woman to *graduate* Georgia Tech.

hanged, hung:

Hanged is a verb meaning "execution by suspending from the neck until dead," as in this example: People are stilled hanged in many countries for committing murders. *Hung* is a verb meaning "to suspend" (not in executions), as in this example: The tapestry was *hung* over the sofa.

hisself:

Hisself is not acceptable as a word. Instead, use *himself* as in this example: He *himself* is aware of his lack of sleep.

if, whether:

If is a conjunction meaning " in the condition that," as in this example: The newspaper column will appear today if there is room for it. *Whether* is a conjunction meaning "alternative possibilities," as in this example: *Whether* Justin flies or

	drives, San Francisco is far from Nashville.
imply, infer:	*Imply* is a verb meaning "to suggest indirectly," as in this example: Dr. Krause *implied* that the final examination will cover every chapter in the textbook. *Infer* is a verb meaning "to arrive at a conclusion," as in this example: Marsha *inferred* from the evidence that the burglar came through the back door.
in regards to:	*In regards to* is a nonstandard expression and should be avoided because the correct terms are *as regards* or *in regard*.
(Incorrect use of *in regards to*):	*In regards to* the bad mid-term grade, Inez feels the the professor forgot to take into account her extra work.
(Correct use of *as regards* or *in regard)*:	*As regards* (in regard) to the bad mid-term grade, Inez feels the professor forgot to take into account her extra work. irregardless: *Irregardless* is not a word. The proper term is *regardless.*
its, it's:	See homonyms in this chapter.
kind of, sort of:	Both these are non-standard expressions. Instead the proper term is *rather,* or delete *kind of* or *sort of* from your writing
(Incorrect):	Mayor Johnson was *kind of* (*sort of*) worried about the city's crime rate.
(Correct):	Mayor Johnson was (rather) worried about the city's crime rate.
lay, lie:	*Lay* is a verb meaning "to put in a certain position," as in this example: *Lay* your head on my shoulder. *Lie* is a verb meaning "to recline in a position of rest," as in this example: Eunice *lies* down after coming back

from work.

leave, let: *Leave* is a verb meaning "to go away," as in this example: The guests will *leave* as soon as their suitcases are inside the trunk of their cars. *Let* is a verb meaning "allow," as in this example: She will let us borrow her laptop computer.

like, such as: *Like* is a preposition meaning "similar to" in comparison to, as in this example: Diana's sister is *like* her older sister. *Such as* is an adjective meaning "specified as an example," as in this example: Bruce has a collection of antique cars *such as* a 1956 Buick and 1948 Ford.

loose, lose: See *loose, lose* in homonyms in this chapter.

may be, maybe: *May be* is a verb meaning "likely to happen," as in this example: Today *may be* the day when we get our clothes from the dry cleaners. *Maybe* is an adverb meaning "possibly," as in this example: *Maybe* the new car will sport a spoiler.

media, medium: *Medium* is a noun meaning "components of mass communication, like newspapers, radio, television, or the Internet," as in this example: As the new medium, the Internet enables people to chat with each other. *Media* is the plural of medium and should be used as such although many people use it as a singular term. The following is an example of the plural form: American *media* make their money from advertising.

off of: *Off of* is nonstandard and should be avoided. The correct form is drop

(Incorrect use of *off of*): the *of* from the expression.

(Correct use *off*): The car rolled *off of* the cliff.

OK, O.K., okay: The car rolled *off* the cliff.
All three are correctly spelled, yet they are not used in standard English.

owing to the fact that: *Owing to the fact that* is a wordy expression. Use *because* instead:

(Incorrect use of *owing to the fact that*): A number of airlines will go out of business *owing to the fact that* gasoline prices are so high.

(Correct use of *because*) : A number of airlines will go out of business *because* gasoline prices are so high.

passed, past: See in homonyms in this chapter.

percent, per cent, percentage: *Percent* also spelled as *per cent* is a noun meaning "a portion of every hundred," as in this example: Sixty *percent* (*per cent*) of the voters elected him as their state representative. *Percentage* is a noun meaning "fraction of one hundred" and is used alone or follows abjectives such as *large* or *small*. An example of the use of *percentage* follows: A small *percentage* of the workers went on a strike.

phenomena: *Phenomena* is a noun meaning "occurrence felt by the senses" and is the plural for of the term phenomenon.

(Plural): Residents are aware of unnatural *phenomena* in this house.

(Singular): Residents are aware of an unnatural *phenomenon* in this house.

plus: *Plus* is a conjunction meaning "added to" and should not be used to join independent clauses.

(Incorrect):	He likes sports cars; plus, he owns a motorcycle, plane, and boat.
(Correct):	He likes sports cars; moreover, he owns a motorcycle, plane, and boat.
precede, proceed:	*Precede* is a verb meaning "to come before," as in this example: The introduction of the musicians will *precede* their performance at the function. *Proceed* is a verb meaning "to move forward," as in this example: We can *proceed* when the traffic signal turns green.
principal, principle:	(See homonyms in this Section.)
quote, quotation:	*Quote* is a verb meaning "to exactly repeat words of another person," as in the example: In his press conference, the U.S. President said, "Please don't *quote* me."
	Quotation is a noun meaning "exact repetition of another person's words," as in this example: Allen began his speech with a *quotation* from William Wordsworth. Note: Avoid using *quote* as an abbreviation of *quotation*. The first one is a verb, and the second one is a noun.
real, really:	*Real* is an adjective meaning "true and real," as in this example: The dish will taste better if you use *real* cheese. *Really* is an adverb meaning "actually." Some use the adjective *real* instead of the adverb *really,* which should be avoided.
(Incorrect use of *real)*	: The principal was *real* upset the students who set the biology lab on fire.
(Correct use of *really*):	The principal was *really* upset at the students who set the biology lab on fire.

(reason is because):	*reason is because* is an improper expression and should be avoided For formal communication and should be avoided. The word *that* should be substituted for *because*.
(Incorrect use of *reason is because*):	The *reason* he bought a new car *is because* his old one needs a new transmission.
(Correct use of *reason is that*):	The *reason* he bought a new car *is that* his old one needs a new transmission.
respectful, respective:	*Respectful* is an adjective meaning "showing deference," as in This example: We have been taught to be respectful of the elders. *Respective* is an adjective meaning "two or more persons or things regarded individually," as in this example: Adrienne's two brothers are successful in their *respective occupations*.
Sensual, sensuous:	*Sensual* is an adjective meaning "gratifying to the sense organs in a sexual manner," as in this example: The exotic dancer evoked *sensual* feelings amongst her audience members. *Sensuous* is an adjective meaning "pleasing to the senses," as in this example: The *sensuous* scent of the candle floated all throughout the house.
set, sit:	*Set* is a verb meaning "to put in a specific place or state," as in this example: A group *set* the wolves free in the wilderness of Wyoming. *Sit* is a verb meaning "to be seated" and does not take an object, as in this example: Juan's house *sits* by the lake.
shall, will:	(See verbs in this Section.)

since:	*Since* is an adverb meaning "between then and now in terms of time" and not to be used instead of *because*.
(Incorrect use of *since*):	Since the police officer was directing traffic, all the drivers were obeying the traffic laws.
(Correct use of *because*):	Because the police officer was directing traffic, all the drivers were obeying the traffic laws.
Some time, sometime. sometimes:	*Some time* is an adjective meaning "a period of time," as in this example: They needed *some time* to complete the project. *Sometime* is an adverb meaning "unstated period in the future," as in this example: Let us have lunch sometime. *Sometimes* as an adverb meaning "at times," as in this example: Sometimes I think about my college days.
suppose to:	*Suppose to* is an incorrect expression. The correct form is *supposed to.*
(Incorrect use of *suppose to*):	The Pennsylvania Department of Transportation was *suppose to* have completed the bridge last winter.
(Correct use of *supposed to*):	The Pennsylvania Department of Transportation was *supposed to* have completed the bridge last winter.
than, then:	*Than* is a conjunction used in comparisons, as in this example: Lucy is taller *than* her husband. *Then* is an adverb meaning "next in order of time," ss in this example: Al told me how he was robbed then he asked me for a loan.
that, which, who:	See pronouns in this chapter. In addition, *that* is used for things,

	animals, collective nouns, or unknown people, as in this example:
(A thing):	The IPod *that* was lost cost three hundred dollars
(An animal):	The horse *that* I rode yesterday is moving to another paddock.
(A collective noun):	The family *that* eats together gets to discuss all their problems.
(An unknown person):	Managers *that* mistreat their employees fail to be good bosses. *Which* is used for animals or things.
(An animal):	Her dog, *which* sleeps all day, whimpers all night.
(A thing):	My radio, *which* is on the desk, can pick up shortwave broadcasts. *Who* is used for people and animals with names.
(A person):	Annette, *who* received a bonus check, bought a plasma television set.
(A named animal):	Lady Regan, who is a poodle, likes to sit on the couch.
theirselves:	*Theirselves* is not acceptable in standard English. The proper term is themselves.
(Incorrect use of *theirselves*):	The children *theirselves* realized that they have to care of the pet.
(Correct use of *themselves*):	The children *themselves* realized that they have to care of the pet.
them:	*Them* is a pronoun functioning as a direct object of a verb and must not be used as adjective.
(Incorrect use of *them*):	*Them* apples look delicious.
(Correct use of *them*):	*Those* apples look delicious.
there, their, they're:	(See homonyms in this Section.)
thru:	Used by commercial enterprises, like fast food restaurants, *thru* is a nonstandard spelling of *through*. Use *through*, not *thru*.
to, too, two:	(See homonyms in this Section).
toward, towards:	Both are used in standard language

	but the preferred one is *toward.*
try and:	*Try and* is nonstandard; substitute *try to.*
(Incorrect use of *try and*):	*Try and* make the birthday cake this afternoon.
(Correct use of *try to*):	*Try and* make the birthday cake this afternoon.
unique:	*Unique* is an adjective meaning "one of a kind" and does not take modifiers such as *very, much, or most.*
(Incorrect):	The most *unique* aspect of the play was the set design.
(Correct):	The *unique* aspect of the play was the set design.
usage, use:	*Usage* is a noun meaning "the way of using something," as in this example: Natural gas *usage* goes up in the winter. *Use* is a verb meaning "to employ," as in this example: John uses his computer every day. The term *usage* should be avoided when the appropriate term is *use.*
(Incorrect use of *usage*):	The *usage* of dictionary is important for all writers.
(Correct use of *use*):	The *use* of dictionary is important for all writers.
use to:	It is *used to*, not *use to.*
(Incorrect use of *use to*):	Marcus *use to* be an air traffic controller.
(Correct use of *used to*):	Marcus *used to* be an air traffic controller.
utilize:	*Utilize* is a verb meaning "to employ" and should not be used in place of *use.*
(Incorrect use of *utilize*):	All students must *utilize* the library to write the research paper.
(Correct use of *use*):	All students must *use* the library to write the research paper.
ways:	*Ways* is nonstandard when it used to mean "path or direction. Use

(Incorrect use of *ways*):	*way.* It is a long *ways* to the mountain cabin.
(Correct use of *way*):	It is a long *way* to the mountain cabin.
weather, whether:	See homonyms in this chapter.
well, good:	See adverbs in this chapter.
who, whom:	*Who* is a pronoun, used to introduce a subject when the antecedent of the clause is a person or persons, as in this example: Those who come to pray will get to play. *Whom* is also a pronoun and used to denote the object, as in this example: The boys, two of *whom* are brothers, played soccer this year.
would of:	*Would of* is a colloquial term and should be avoided. Use *would have* instead.
(Incorrect use of *would of*):	Gene *would of* gone shopping if Cynthia gave him his money.
(Correct use of *would have*):	Gene *would have* gone shopping if Cynthia gave him his money.
you:	See point of view in this chapter.
your, you're:	See homonyms in this chapter.

ERRORS CHART

Your name _____

Transfer errors from this sheet to the chart in your syllabus or workbook

CHECKLIST OF SPECIFIC SENTENCE-LEVEL ERRORS

	Essay #1	Essay #2	Essay 3	Essay #4	Essay #5	Essay #6	Essay #7
1 Awkward, unclear sentences							
2 Short, choppy sentences							
3 Sentence fragments							
4 Comma splice/run-on/ fused sentences							
5 Subject/verb agreement							
6 Tense shift (use present tense with literature)							
7 Person shift (first to second, etc.)							
8 Pronouncement agreement							
9 Parallel structure							
10 Word choice/diction							
11 Comma use (learn comma rules)							
12 Semi-colon/colon use							
13 Apostrophe use							
14 Capitalization							
15 Spelling (use spell check in your head, not computer)							
16 Punctuation of quotations							
17 Underline titles of books and films							

Your name _____

PAGE 2

CHECKLIST OF SPECIFIC SENTENCE-LEVEL ERRORS

avoid....

	Essay #1	Essay #2	Essay 3	Essay #4	Essay #5	Essay #6	Essay #7
1 beginning sentences with coordinating conjunctions							
2 overuse of expletive constructions							
3 casual asides, slang terms							
4 trite words like "nice" "cute" and "thing"							
5 using second person "you" and "your" etc.							
6 telling us about something rather than *showing*							
7 abstractions and universals general terms, etc.							
8 pretentious or overwritten passages, sound forced							
9 unreal images, forced comparisons, weak similes							
10 quotes or slangs words or too many jargon words							
11 colloquial diction (too casual)							
12 Under developed or week paragraphs							
13 formal announcements or direct statements							
14 omitted page numbers							
15 incorrect quotation use or citation method							
16 other _____							

Index

The Author

Niaz Khan teaches at Clark Atlanta University in Atlanta. He received his B.A. and M.A. degrees in English from Lambuth University and Ohio University respectively. In 1991, he earned his Ph.D. degree in communication from The University of Southern Mississippi. His writings have appeared in books, journals, magazines, and newspapers. For a number of years, he was a book reviewer for *The Jackson* (Tenn.) *Sun* and a columnist for *The Tuscaloosa* (Alabama) *News* and The New York Times Regional Wire Service. In addition, he has been recognized many times for his teaching—including receiving the faculty of the year award.

ERRORS CHART

Your name_____

Transfer errors from this sheet to the chart in your syllabus or workbook

CHECKLIST OF SPECIFIC SENTENCE-LEVEL ERRORS

	Essay #1	Essay #2	Essay 3	Essay #4	Essay #5	Essay #6	Essay #7
1 Awkward, unclear sentences							
2 Short, choppy sentences							
3 Sentence fragments							
4 Comma splice/run-on/ fused sentences							
5 Subject/verb agreement							
6 Tense shift (use present tense with literature)							
7 Person shift (first to second, etc.)							
8 Pronouncement agreement							
9 Parallel structure							
10 Word choice/diction							
11 Comma use (learn comma rules)							
12 Semi-colon/colon use							
13 Apostrophe use							
14 Capitalization							
15 Spelling (use spell check in your head, not computer)							
16 Punctuation of quotations							
17 Underline titles of books and films							

CHECKLIST OF SPECIFIC SENTENCE-LEVEL ERRORS

avoid....

	Essay #1	Essay #2	Essay 3	Essay #4	Essay #5	Essay #6	Essay #7
1 beginning sentences with coordinating conjunctions							
2 overuse of expletive constructions							
3 casual asides, slang terms							
4 trite words like "nice" "cute" and "thing"							
5 using second person "you" and "your" etc.							
6 telling us about something rather than *showing*							
7 abstractions and universals general terms, etc.							
8 pretentious or overwritten passages, sound forced							
9 unreal images, forced comparisons, weak similes							
10 quotes or slangs words or too many jargon words							
11 colloquial diction (too casual)							
12 Under developed or week paragraphs							
13 formal announcements or direct statements							
14 omitted page numbers							
15 incorrect quotation use or citation method							
16 other _____ _____							

ERRORS CHART

Your name_____

Transfer errors from this sheet to the chart in your syllabus or workbook

CHECKLIST OF SPECIFIC SENTENCE-LEVEL ERRORS

	Essay #1	Essay #2	Essay 3	Essay #4	Essay #5	Essay #6	Essay #7
1 Awkward, unclear sentences							
2 Short, choppy sentences							
3 Sentence fragments							
4 Comma splice/run-on/ fused sentences							
5 Subject/verb agreement							
6 Tense shift *(use present tense with literature)*							
7 Person shift *(first to second, etc.)*							
8 Pronouncement agreement							
9 Parallel structure							
10 Word choice/diction							
11 Comma use *(learn comma rules)*							
12 Semi-colon/colon use							
13 Apostrophe use							
14 Capitalization							
15 Spelling *(use spell check in your head, not computer)*							
16 Punctuation of quotations							
17 Underline titles of books and films							

121

CHECKLIST OF SPECIFIC SENTENCE-LEVEL ERRORS

avoid....

	Essay #1	Essay #2	Essay 3	Essay #4	Essay #5	Essay #6	Essay #7
1 beginning sentences with coordinating conjunctions							
2 overuse of expletive constructions							
3 casual asides, slang terms							
4 trite words like "nice" "cute" and "thing"							
5 using second person "you" and "your" etc.							
6 telling us about something rather than *showing*							
7 abstractions and universals general terms, etc.							
8 pretentious or overwritten passages, sound forced							
9 unreal images, forced comparisons, weak similes							
10 quotes or slangs words or too many jargon words							
11 colloquial diction (too casual)							
12 Under developed or week paragraphs							
13 formal announcements or direct statements							
14 omitted page numbers							
15 incorrect quotation use or citation method							
16 other _____ _____							

ERRORS CHART

Your name _____

Transfer errors from this sheet to the chart in your syllabus or workbook

CHECKLIST OF SPECIFIC SENTENCE-LEVEL ERRORS

	Essay #1	Essay #2	Essay 3	Essay #4	Essay #5	Essay #6	Essay #7
1 Awkward, unclear sentences							
2 Short, choppy sentences							
3 Sentence fragments							
4 Comma splice/run-on/ fused sentences							
5 Subject/verb agreement							
6 Tense shift (use present tense with literature)							
7 Person shift (first to second, etc.)							
8 Pronouncement agreement							
9 Parallel structure							
10 Word choice/diction							
11 Comma use (learn comma rules)							
12 Semi-colon/colon use							
13 Apostrophe use							
14 Capitalization							
15 Spelling (use spell check in your head, not computer)							
16 Punctuation of quotations							
17 Underline titles of books and films							

123

CHECKLIST OF SPECIFIC SENTENCE-LEVEL ERRORS

avoid....

	Essay #1	Essay #2	Essay 3	Essay #4	Essay #5	Essay #6	Essay #7
1 beginning sentences with coordinating conjunctions							
2 overuse of expletive constructions							
3 casual asides, slang terms							
4 trite words like "nice" "cute" and "thing"							
5 using second person "you" and "your" etc.							
6 telling us about something rather than *showing*							
7 abstractions and universals general terms, etc.							
8 pretentious or overwritten passages, sound forced							
9 unreal images, forced comparisons, weak similes							
10 quotes or slangs words or too many jargon words							
11 colloquial diction (too casual)							
12 Under developed or week paragraphs							
13 formal announcements or direct statements							
14 omitted page numbers							
15 incorrect quotation use or citation method							
16 other _____ _____							